COMPARISON GRAPHIC ORGANIZER

DIRECTIONS: In the gray ovals, write the two things you want to compare. In the middle ovals, write the things about them that are alike. On the side ovals, write the things that are different. Draw more ovals if you need to. On the lines at the bottom, write examples of the correct use of A and B.

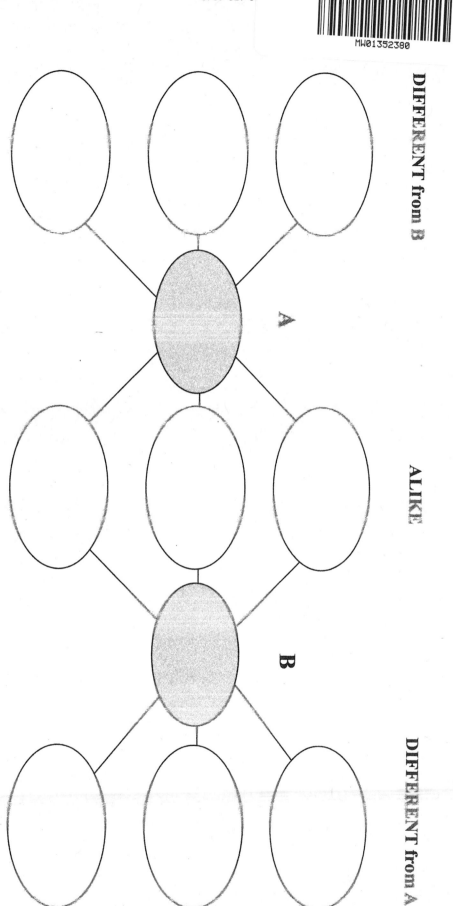

DIFFERENT from B   ALIKE   DIFFERENT from A

Tuning Up English With Logic

THE LANGUAGE MECHANIC

Written by
M. A. Hockett

© 2001
THE CRITICAL THINKING CO.™
www.CriticalThinking.com
Phone: 800 458 4849 • Fax: 831-393-3277
P.O. Box 1610 • Seaside • CA 93955-1610
ISBN 978-0-89455-761-3

Reproduction of This Copyrighted Material
The intellectual material in this product is the copyrighted property of The Critical Thinking Co.™ The individual or entity who initially purchased this product from The Critical Thinking Co.™ or one of its authorized resellers is licensed to reproduce (print or duplicate on paper) up to 35 copies of each page in this product per year for use within one home or one classroom. Our copyright and this limited reproduction permission (user) agreement strictly prohibit the sale of any of the copyrighted material in this product. Any reproduction beyond these expressed limits is strictly prohibited without the written permission of The Critical Thinking Co.™ Please visit http://www.criticalthinking.com/copyright for more information. The Critical Thinking Co.™ retains full intellectual property rights on all its products (eBooks, books, and software).
Printed in the United States of America by Edwards Brothers Malloy, Inc., Ann Arbor, MI (June 2013)

Many thanks to the following educators:

Jeff Cassidy	Britta Montes
Elaine Barbour	Linda Barbour
Carole Bannes	Cheryl Block

TABLE OF CONTENTS

INTRODUCTION v
   Purpose of the Book v
   Using the Book v
   Teacher Help vi
   Preparing the Lesson vii
   Presenting the Lesson vii
   Reinforcement vii
   Unit Notes viii
   Comparison Graphic Organizer xi

UNIT 1: CAPITALIZATION 1
   Proper Nouns: Names of People 1
   Proper Nouns: Names of Places and Things 5
   Proper Adjectives 8
   UNIT REVIEW: Capitalization 11

UNIT 2: RUN-ONS AND FRAGMENTS 12
   Run-On Sentences 12
   Interjections 15
   Direct Quotations 18
   Sentence Fragments 21
   UNIT REVIEW: Run-Ons and Fragments 23

UNIT 3: PRONOUNS 24
   Pronouns as Subject and Object 24
   Possessive Pronouns 27
   First Person Last 29
   UNIT REVIEW: Pronouns 31

UNIT 4: MODIFIERS 32
   Adjectives and Adverbs 32
   Comparative/Superlative Modifiers 36
   Articles: A, An 38
   Articles: A and The with General & Specific Nouns 40
   Misplaced Modifiers 42
   UNIT REVIEW: Modifiers 45

UNIT 5: VERBS 46
   Past, Present, and Future Tense 46
   Irregular Verb Forms 48
   Parallel Construction for Tense 51
   Helping Verbs 53
   Linking Verbs 55
   UNIT REVIEW: Verbs 57

UNIT 6: AGREEMENT 58
   Pronoun/Antecedent Agree in Gender 58
   Pronoun/Antecedent Agree in Number 61
   Noun or Pronoun/Verb Agree in Number 63

Adjective/Noun Agree in Number 66
Adjectives (This, That)/Noun Agree in Space or Time 68
UNIT REVIEW: Agreement 71

UNIT 7: UNNECESSARY WORDS 72
Double Negatives 72
Noun or Pronoun (Not Both) as Subject 74
Here/There with This/That 76
UNIT REVIEW: Unnecessary Words 78

UNIT 8: PUNCTUATION ' ? ! " " 79
Apostrophe: Contractions 79
Apostrophe with Singular Possessive 82
Apostrophe with Plural Possessive 85
Question Mark 88
Exclamation Mark 90
Quotation Marks 92
UNIT REVIEW: Punctuation 94

UNIT 9: PUNCTUATION: Comma 95
Comma in a Series 95
Commas to Set Off the Year 98
Comma in Address 101
Comma After State 104
Comma with Noun of Address 106
Comma to Separate Quotation from Speaker 108
Comma After Introductory Words 112
Comma with Conjunctions 115
Comma with Appositives—Words that Explain 118
Comma with Introductory Dependent Clause 121
UNIT REVIEW: Comma 124

UNIT 10: FRIENDLY LETTER: Greeting and Closing 126
Capitals and Punctuation in Greeting (and Body) 126
Capitals and Punctuation in Closing (and Body) 127
UNIT REVIEW: Friendly Letter 130

UNIT 11: SPELLING AND VOCABULARY 131
Confused Word Pairs 131
Homophones and Other Similar Words 134
Spelling Plural and Singular Nouns 138
Silent Consonants 141
Silent E for Long Vowels 144
Consonant Doubling with -ing or -ed 146
UNIT REVIEW: Spelling and Vocabulary 148

GLOSSARY 151
ANSWER KEY 157
SAMPLE ACTIVITY 172

INTRODUCTION

Our language is the vehicle we use to carry our messages. Without a mechanic to keep it running smoothly, that vehicle can run into problems. The messages can become murky or misdirected. Communication can break down if the parts are not operating correctly. Your students must act as mechanics—and not only as mechanics but also as detectives—detectives who know the rules and pay close attention to clues and the logic of their language.

Is there any logic to the rules for grammar? Yes! Though not always obvious, the language rules are based on logic. If students are not vigilant about these rules and their logic, unintended meanings can sneak into our messages!

Purpose of the Book

The Language Mechanic helps make learning fun by offering a humorous slant on the subject of grammar through comical examples of incorrect usage, plus exercises with a logic twist. The book not only teaches basic rules of language mechanics, it reinforces the rules by showing the logic behind them. It illustrates the confusing, absurd, and humorous results of breaking them. It shows examples and gives practice in applying the rules.

This book also introduces the concepts used in The Critical Thinking Company's™ *Editor in Chief*® series, levels A and B. Therefore, it is appropriate instruction and practice before testing understanding with the *Editor in Chief*® exercises. For quick, fun practice activities, order The Critical Thinking Company's™ *Punctuation Puzzlers*™ (see sample, p. 172).

Using the Book

The book gives instruction, examples, and practice on specific rules of grammar, punctuation, capitalization, usage, vocabulary, and spelling. Each rule is presented as a lesson with three parts: an introduction to the rule, Your Turn exercises, and Challenge exercises.

The introductory page of each lesson includes the following:

- The "Grabber"—an example of miscommunication that illustrates the need for the rule
- The Logic—why the rule makes sense
- The Rule—an explanation of the rule and how to use it
- Practice exercises—several exercises to prepare the student for independent practice exercises (Your Turn)

Your Turn problems include a variety of exercises (matching, select, fill in the blank, editing); many require the use of context clues and logic combined with knowledge of the language rule.

Challenge exercises are designed for those students who are ready for a level of thinking that is a little beyond that of Your Turn exercises.

Each unit includes one or more paragraphs for editing as reinforcement after the lessons of the unit are completed.

Note that the lessons are grouped more by logic than by conventional organization. For example, the use of quotation marks to enclose quotations is included in the unit on Run-ons and Fragments. That's because the logic of their use is based on separating the spoken word from those surrounding it. If not separated, the quotation can run on with other words, causing confusion.

Read the Unit Notes in the Teacher Help section below for information on each Unit and its lessons (see also the Table of Contents).

Teacher Help

You will need a sense of humor with this book (be forewarned that there may be some groaners here and there). Encourage students to play with words—show them that language can be fun!

Emphasize to students that they must act not only as mechanics to fix errors but also as detectives to uncover errors; they must use context clues and the logic of the sentences to figure out the meaning. But they need to watch out! Sometimes the context clues can be subtle, especially in Challenge questions. Even you, the teacher, may need to be especially careful in reading.

You may use the lessons as sequenced or in an order that fits your instructional needs. The included Glossary may be especially helpful to students in this case. Whatever lesson you do, look it over in advance. That way, you can anticipate potential trouble spots and plan on spending the time your students will need for complete understanding. You may want to select one or more questions per lesson for discussion. Challenge questions can be especially good for this; you may also want to assign variations of Challenge questions as assignments to be written on an extra piece of paper.

It may seem that there are more exercises than you need in some lessons. Just pick the ones you feel will be most valuable for the time you have available. Similarly, if there are a few lessons for rules that your students are not required to learn or are not ready for, you may wish to skip them.

Preparing the Lesson

Read the Unit Notes (page vii) for specific lessons before teaching each lesson.

Before doing a lesson, go over any terms you think the students need to review. The Glossary (page 151) is included for students' reference. You may copy and distribute the glossary so students have access to definitions while doing lessons. Have extra paper available for student use. You may find it helpful to enlarge the lesson on a photocopy machine before recopying and distributing, especially for younger learners.

Presenting the Lesson

1. Display the example at the top of the lesson page, the Logic, and the Rule for the whole group to see. Discuss the difference in meaning between what the writer says and what the reader thinks. After reading the Rule, have students read and answer the first Practice exercise. Go over the answer together with the students. Make sure they understand why the answer given is best. Finish the rest of the Practice section in the same way.

   Teacher-led group activities enable communication growth as a result of the interchange of viewpoints. Students may interpret the same sentences in different ways. This difference helps illustrate to students the importance of agreeing on and abiding by exact rules in their writing.

2. After you are confident that students understand the rule, have them do Your Turn exercises. From Your Turn and Challenge sections, assign only as many exercises as your students can do without frustration. Students who finish early with no problems may be encouraged to further explore the Challenge questions.

3. In a similar way, give the remaining lessons for the unit, each on a different day. A day or two after the unit is complete, briefly review what was learned, and then assign the Unit Review.

Reinforcement

The following are general suggestions for reinforcement of unit lessons. (For suggestions relevant to specific units, see Unit Notes, on the next page.) You may have the students do the following: draw a picture to illustrate the intended meaning (shown next to the words "You mean") at the beginning of each lesson; make up their own exercises and trade with each other; fill in the graphic organizer chart on page xii (compare and contrast two elements); write their own examples showing how breaking the rule results in a different meaning (requires lots of thinking!); use *Editor in Chief*® (available from Critical Thinking Co.™, www.CriticalThinking.com) exercises as a starting point to create and discuss new examples illustrating the rule, or as further practice for applying the rules in context.

Unit Notes

Below are notes specific to each unit, including terms to preview first with students and suggestions for further reinforcement. Note that there is no unit designated specifically for nouns. The logical rules concerning nouns are included in other units, such as Capitalization, Agreement, and Spelling and Vocabulary.

Unit 1 – Capitalization (p. 1)

TERMS: adjective, capitalize, noun, proper adjective, proper noun

COMMENTS

- For capitalization in friendly letters, see Unit 10, Friendly Letter.
- For capitalization used at the beginning of a sentence, see Unit 2, Run-Ons and Fragments.
- Photocopy the Capitalizing Proper Nouns chart on page 2. Distribute it to students to use while completing the first two lessons. (They will fill in the Persons section in the first lesson and the Places and Things in the second lesson.)
- Photocopy the Capitalizing Proper Adjectives chart on page 9 for students to fill out during the Proper Adjectives lesson on page 8.

EXTENSIONS: Give students stories or articles from newspapers and magazines; have them highlight all proper nouns and adjectives. Discuss why they are proper. Give a list of proper nouns and adjectives and have students sort by category: proper noun as person, place, or thing OR proper adjective.

Unit 2 – Run-Ons and Fragments (p. 12)

TERMS: capitalize, direct quotation, ending punctuation, exclamation, exclamation mark, interjection, quotation, quotation marks, run-on, sentence, split quotation

COMMENTS

- This unit includes interjections and direct quotations because if the given rule is not followed, the meaning runs together with surrounding ideas.

EXTENSIONS: Students intentionally write confusing run-ons and fragments, along with hints to suggest correct meaning; partners trade and correct. Give examples and discuss possible meanings to help them start: "She shouted loudly over the noise they heard her." OR "The boys were shy. And quiet. Girls were shouting at them."

Unit 3 – Pronouns (p. 24)

TERMS: first person, noun, object, possessive pronoun, pronoun, subject

EXTENSIONS: Students use subject/object pronouns correctly in sentences: I thanked her. Then use double subjects and double objects: He gave it to her and me. She and he gave it to us. Use each possessive pronoun pair in sentences: My mother likes that car. I like mine.

Unit 4 – Modifiers (p. 32)

TERMS: adjective, adjective phrase, adverb, adverb phrase, article, comparative and superlative forms, definite article, indefinite article, misplaced modifier, noun, positive modifier, syllables, verb

COMMENTS
- This unit includes lessons on articles because articles are adjectives.
- This unit includes a lesson on misplaced modifiers. If your students are not ready for this concept, omit the lesson.

Unit 5 – Verbs (p. 46)

TERMS: action verb, future tense, helping verb, irregular verb, linking verb, parallel tense, past tense, plain verb, present tense, tense, verb

EXTENSIONS: Fill in a comparison graphic organizer (page xi) for comparing and contrasting any two tenses (past, present, future), regular vs. irregular tense, linking vs. action verbs, or helping vs. main verbs. Students draw cartoons to illustrate tenses from a simple story sequence that other students make up.

Unit 6 – Agreement (p. 58)

TERMS: adjective, antecedent, gender, noun, plural, pronoun, singular

EXTENSIONS: Using stories from any available story or text, students highlight and label each pair of words that agree as follows: pronoun/antecedent, noun/verb, and adjective/noun.

Unit 7 – Unnecessary Words (p. 72)

TERMS: adverb, negative, noun, phrase, pronoun, subject

EXTENSIONS: Students write sentences containing unnecessary words from each lesson category; partners trade papers and cross out unnecessary words.

Unit 8 – Punctuation ' ? ! " " (p. 79)

TERMS: apostrophe, contraction, exclamation, exclamation mark, plural possessive, possessive, question, question mark, quotation marks

COMMENTS

- This unit includes punctuation other than commas and periods. (The comma has its own unit, following this one. Using a period is addressed in the Run-Ons and Fragments unit.)

EXTENSIONS: On copies of the comparison graphic organizer (page xi), compare and contrast any two kinds of punctuation. Also, contrast singular possessives with plural possessives OR plural possessives ending in "s" with plural possessives not ending in "s."

Unit 9 – Punctuation: Comma (p. 95)

TERMS: appositive, clause, conjunction, dependent clause, exclamation, independent clause, introductory dependent clause, introductory word, noun of address, question, quotation, series

EXTENSIONS: Students create sentences or stories without commas for other students to correct. Compare and contrast dependent and independent clauses on a comparison graphic organizer.

Unit 10 – Friendly Letter: Greeting, Closing (p. 126)

TERMS: capitalize, closing, comma, greeting, noun of address

EXTENSIONS: Students write letters. Topic suggestions are: tell a friend you're moving; ask for help with a project; thank someone for a gift.

Unit 11 – Spelling and Vocabulary (p. 131)

TERMS: consonant, homophones, plural, singular noun, vowel

COMMENTS

- Confused Word Pairs includes definitions of confused word pairs.
- Silent Consonants includes a list of definitions of words with silent consonants.
- Silent E for Long Vowels includes a list of definitions of words with long vowels.

EXTENSIONS: Students write confused words and homophones correctly in sentences of their own. Compare and contrast pairs of words on comparison graphic organizers (see page xi).

COMPARISON GRAPHIC ORGANIZER

DIRECTIONS: In the gray ovals, write the two things you want to compare. In the middle ovals, write the things about them that are alike. In the side ovals, write the things that are different. Draw more ovals if you need to. On the lines at the bottom, write examples of the correct use of A and B.

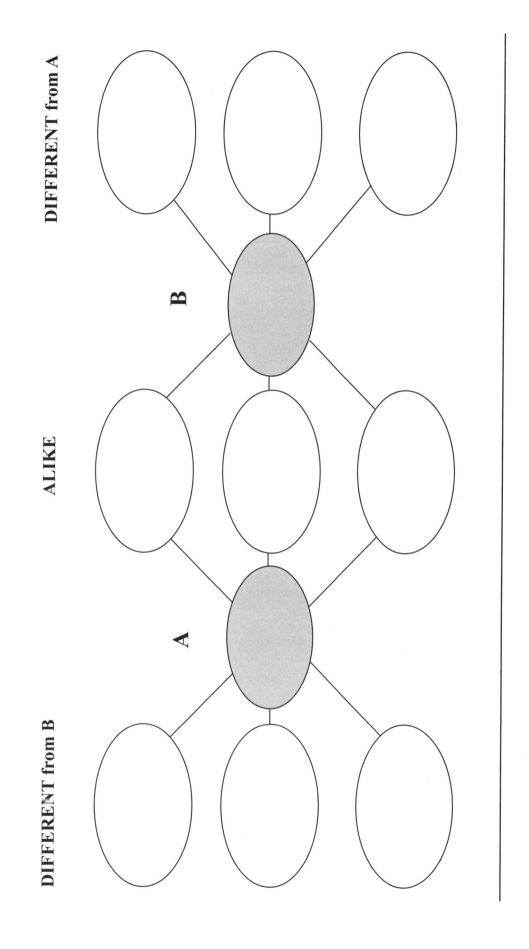

1. CAPITALIZATION

Proper Nouns: Names of People

You and Andy Gray were so scared you both became pale.

You write: We saw a ghost! That made Andy gray and me white.

Readers think: Andy was the color gray!

You mean: We saw a ghost! That made Andy *Gray* and me white.

> **THE LOGIC**
> If a person's name has no capital, readers cannot tell that it is a name. They may read it as a different part of speech.
>
> **RULE 1**
> Capitalize any words used as part of a person's name, including titles.
> - J.G. Smith
> - Stretch
> - Doctor Adams
> - President Cutter
> - Dad
> - Dr. Smith
> - Aunt Mary
> - Mrs. Kathy White
>
> **RULE 2**
> Do not capitalize the general term for a name: the *doctor,* my *dad*

PRACTICE

1. Review the examples for "Persons" on the noun chart on page 2. Add your own examples of names that do or do not need capitals.

2. Match each sentence below to the clue that describes it. Write the number of the correct clue in the blanks.

   Clue 1: Amy is unhappy.

   Clue 2: Amy's last name is a color word.

   a. *Mad Monsters* was such a sad movie that it made Amy blue. _____

   b. Many people were really robots created by Dr. Malice. In fact, he made Amy Brown. _____

CAPITALIZING PROPER NOUNS

Look at the chart as you do each lesson. Fill in each section with the names of persons, places, or things that you know. Use examples that are different from those given.

TYPE OF NOUNS	CAPITALIZE (specific persons, places, or things)	DO NOT CAPITALIZE (general persons, places, or things)
PERSONS	Sis Aunt Sally Curly Dr. Jones Mrs. Claymore _____ _____ _____ _____	my sister your aunt my friend the doctor his wife _____ _____ _____ _____
PLACES	Forest Grove Park Smith College Brazil Nile Valley _____ _____ _____ _____	the park over there the university eastern country river valley _____ _____ _____ _____
THINGS (includes objects, ideas, titles, days of month, etc.)	Eiffel Tower Mona Lisa Wrigley Field Fourth of July September "Jingle Bells" _____ _____	a tower a famous painting a baseball park a holiday a month a song _____ _____

The Language Mechanic | Capitalization

YOUR TURN

1. In each blank, write the number of the clue that describes the sentence.

   Clue 1: The company is part of an army.

   Clue 2: The company is a bakery.

   a. Here's the company's general baker. _____

   b. Here's the company's General Baker. _____

   Clue 1: Ms. Woods was beginning to understand army life.

   Clue 2: The sun was rising over the trees.

   c. It was dawning on private woods. _____

   d. It was dawning on Private Woods. _____

2. Using context and logic, circle the word that makes sense in each sentence.

   a. You've been sitting still too long, so you'll walk to your friend's place. What do you say to her?

   I'll see you and (Stretch, stretch) my legs.

   b. You will visit Jake and his friend. His friend has a funny nickname because he is tall. What might you say to Jake?

   I'll visit you and (Stretch, stretch), your friend.

3. Underline any name that needs to be capitalized.

   Hello, solon. This woman's name is smoky. She is our club president. Please show president smoky where my mom is sitting. I know dad would love to meet her, too.

The Language Mechanic   Capitalization

CHALLENGE

1. Circle the correct word in parentheses. (Hint: See "Comma with Appositives" on page 118.)

    a. Cordova, I want you to meet someone. This is (president, President) Cutler.

    b. Cordova, I want you to meet someone. This is our (president, President), Cutler.

2. A letter in one of the following sentences should be capitalized. Underline it.

    a. I think the letters g and h were there, but i was not.

    b. I think the letters g and h were there, but i was not sure.

3. Either answer could make sense in the following sentence. Explain why.

    Stretch Road seems to go on forever. It's a long _____. (Stretch, stretch)

    _____

    _____

    _____

The Language Mechanic · Capitalization

Proper Nouns: Names of Places and Things

You think the month after February will be very cold.

You write: We will have a hard march.

Readers think: You will be marching with difficulty!

You mean: We will have a hard *March*.

> **THE LOGIC**
> Leaving off the capital can give the reader the wrong message. The word *march* is a word for "walk," as well as a name for a month (which should be capitalized).
>
> **RULE 1**
> Capitalize the important words in the name for a specific place or thing.
>
> **RULE 2**
> Don't capitalize a general place or thing (words like *tower, state, month*).
>
> - St. Augustine   • Eiffel Tower   • Sunday   • *Charlotte's Web*
> - Brazil   • U.C.L.A   • November   • "Home on the Range"

PRACTICE

1. Review the examples for "Places" and "Things" on the noun chart on page 2. Add your own examples of places and things that do or do not need capitals.

2. Underline any place or thing that needs to be capitalized.

    Our choir traveled to many places last year. We went to texas and florida in november. In january, we went to italy and saw the tower of pisa. We sang in st. paul's cathedral. By then we were ready to return to hampton college.

3. Read the clue. Circle the word that makes sense in each sentence.

    Clue: We visited many countries to see dinnerware.

    a. We think (China, china) was the most interesting. We also liked Russia and Taiwan.

    b. We think (China, china) was the most interesting. The patterns were lovely.

The Language Mechanic   Capitalization

YOUR TURN

1. In each blank, write the number of the clue that describes the sentence.

   Clue 1: We showed her a newspaper.

   Clue 2: We told her the times of the races.

   a. She asked when the races started, so we gave her the times. _____

   b. She asked when the races started, so we gave her the Times. _____

2. Read the clue. Circle the word that makes sense in each sentence.

   Clue: Some brave person was leading the people through the hurricane.

   a. That was a (major storm, Major Storm) that destroyed many homes.

   b. That was (major storm, Major Storm). He saved them from the storm.

3. Circle all nouns that should be capitalized.

   We clean house on our cleaning day. We stay in on a rainy day and go out on a sunny day. We relax on a sunday and work on a friday.

   Explain why you circled each word.

   _____

   _____

4. For each sentence, circle the words that make sense.

   a. Our phone wires came down when the (north pole, North Pole) was hit by a car. That stopped our TV program about the trip to the (north pole, North Pole).

   b. We had many (pleasant times, Pleasant Times) reading the daily (pleasant times, Pleasant Times).

   c. We'll (dance up a storm, Dance Up a Storm) when we hear (dance up a storm, Dance Up a Storm) on the CD.

   d. We were (all fired up, All Fired Up) to watch (all fired up, All Fired Up) at the arena.

CHALLENGE

1. In each blank, write the number of the clue that describes the sentence.

    Clue 1: We were dancing to a piece of banjo music.

    Clue 2: We were scared when the car stopped on a cloudy night in the Rockies.

    a. We were sweating over the Foggy Mountain Breakdown. _____

    b. We were sweating over the foggy mountain breakdown. _____

2. Circle each proper noun. Cross out its first letter and write a capital.

    a. They had four boring trips in the third month. Those trips made their march routine.

    b. They practiced several patterns for the july parade. Those moves made up their march routine.

3. Circle all words that need capitals. Explain why you circled each one.

    Friday is fish day, thursday is ground beef day, and Monday is groundhog day.

    _____

    _____

    _____

The Language Mechanic   Capitalization

Proper Adjectives

His Red Cross team works in the country.

You write: He is on the red cross country team.

Readers think: His cross-country team is the red team.

You mean: He is on the Red Cross country team.

> **THE LOGIC**
>
> Leaving the capital off a proper adjective or part of a proper adjective can confuse or mislead the reader. Putting a capital on an adjective that is *not* proper can also give a wrong meaning.
>
> **THE RULE**
>
> Use a capital for each word of a proper adjective. Proper adjectives describe specific nouns. *Italy*, a specific place, is a proper noun. *Italian*, a word describing things from Italy, is a proper adjective. Look on page 9 for other examples of proper adjectives.

PRACTICE

1. Review the examples for "Proper Adjectives" on the chart on page 9. Add your own examples of adjectives that do and do not change spelling.

2. Underline each word used as a proper adjective. Write a capital letter above it. Find the noun that is modified by the proper adjective and circle it. The first example is done for you.

   Example: They attended the <u>olympic</u> (event). [O above "olympic"]

   a. The martian battle was fantastic. Many outsiders invaded the planet Mars.

   b. Whoever finds something good will store it for later. Find it at a goodwill store.

3. The following sentences are capitalized correctly. Underline the sentence that shows what state the cow is from. (Hint: Jerseys and Holsteins are kinds of cows.)

   a. We got a new Jersey cow and an old Holstein cow.

   b. We got a New Jersey cow and a Wisconsin chicken.

CAPITALIZING PROPER ADJECTIVES

Some proper nouns can be used as they are to form proper adjectives. Their spelling doesn't change. Some proper nouns change spelling to create adjectives. Read the examples below. Add more proper adjectives and nouns to fit each example.

PROPER NOUNS	PROPER ADJECTIVES (from <u>nouns</u> that don't change spelling)
Sunday Viking New York	<u>Sunday</u> dinner <u>Viking</u> ships <u>New York</u> pizza

PROPER NOUNS	PROPER ADJECTIVES (from <u>nouns</u> that do change spelling)
France Mars Olympus	a loaf of <u>French</u> bread a <u>Martian</u> battle an <u>Olympic</u> athlete

The Language Mechanic Capitalization

YOUR TURN

1. In each blank, write the number of the clue that describes the sentence.

   Clue 1: The hotel is named York, and it is not old.

   Clue 2: The hotel is named after a state.

   a. We stayed at the new York hotel. _____

   b. We stayed at the New York hotel. _____

2. Fill in the blank with a proper adjective so the sentence is true for you!

   a. The author has a February birthday. I have a(n) _____ birthday.

   b. She is a California citizen. I am a(n) _____ citizen.

3. Circle any proper adjective and write its capital letter above the word.

   a. Our mothers may cruise or take a hawaiian tour.

   b. I cancelled my father's june cruise, but not my mother's may cruise.

CHALLENGE

1. Underline each word below that should be capitalized. Remember to use context and logic!

   a. There have been three july parties. It's nearly August, and we are having the fourth of the july celebrations.

   b. There are many parties on Independence Day. They are the fourth of july celebrations.

UNIT REVIEW: Capitalization

Read the following story and circle each word that needs a capital letter.

On a monday in june, my sister and I went to ratland, Mouse-achusetts. Nan and i wore ears and whiskers. We had to watch out for catzilla, the beastly cat. We tried to get all the Muenster cheese without getting too full to climb. We went up a small model of the statue of liberty. It was near rattan Island. We were part of a new movie called mousetrap. It will be released next september 15.

We thought it was great to be away from school! Then we saw principal ryan. He was eating Swiss cheese with french fries while we ran the maze. He said we should visit rodent run college in ratland. We did! In the art department, we created a painting called mousa lisa. In the music department, we played home on the mousepad.

Mice sure do have a lot of fun!

2. RUN-ONS AND FRAGMENTS

Run-On Sentences

The ice-cream man stopped at the pool and left the ice cream in the sun. He dove in the pool. The ice cream in the truck melted.

You write: He dove in the ice cream in the truck was melted glop.

Readers think: He dove in the ice cream. In the truck was melted glop.

You mean: He dove in. *The* ice cream in the truck was melted glop.

THE LOGIC

Leaving out the boundaries between sentences confuses the reader. It is not clear which words go with which sentence.

THE RULE

Separate sentences to communicate clearly. Use a capital at the beginning, place ending punctuation after the first complete thought, and start a new sentence with a capital letter.

PRACTICE

1. Add a period, cross out the lowercase letter, and add a capital to show where sentences should be divided. Make exactly two sentences for each line. The first one is done for you.

    a. We watch the man as he runs. ~~h~~He gets tired quickly.

    b. She gave me a watch that works I know the right time.

    c. I thought it was noon when will we be going?

2. Add a period and capital only where needed. Think about the meaning!

    a. The man runs as long as he has energy he gets tired quickly.

    b. The doctor got rid of the pain that makes me feel good.

    c. She hates that bully. He took her stuffed bear that makes her feel good.

The Language Mechanic   Run-Ons and Fragments

YOUR TURN

1. Make each run-on into exactly two sentences by crossing out the lowercase letter and adding a capital and a period. The first one is done for you.

   a. I have a turtle~~.~~ ~~i~~**I**t loves to swim.

   b. She drove around the town seemed large.

   c. She drove around town she was lost.

   d. She has a car we love to drive it.

   e. She has a car we love to drive it is fast.

2. Below is a run-on sentence. Circle the letter that shows the best way to fix it according to the clue.

   The day is sunny and warm birds glide lazily in the sky.

   Clue: The birds are NOT warm.

   a. The day is sunny. Warm birds glide lazily in the sky.

   b. The day is sunny and. Warm birds glide lazily in the sky.

   c. The day is sunny and warm. Birds glide lazily in the sky.

3. Below is a run-on sentence. Circle the letter that shows the best way to fix it.

   She crawled on the ground, and she surprised a grasshopper and it jumped high, and it landed on her nose.

   a. She crawled on the ground. And she surprised a grasshopper and it jumped high, and it landed on her nose.

   b. She crawled on the ground, and she surprised a grasshopper. It jumped high, and it landed on her nose.

   c. She crawled on the ground, and she surprised a grasshopper. And It jumped high, and it landed on her nose.

   d. She crawled on the ground, and she surprised a grasshopper and it jumped high. It landed on her nose.

The Language Mechanic   Run-Ons and Fragments

CHALLENGE

1. Make each run-on into two sentences by adding a period and a capital.

    a. We played with the fish we fed the monsters at noon.

    b. We played with the fish that we fed the monsters we ate, too.

    c. I thought Thursday would never come on Wednesday I was excited.

    d. She said Thanksgiving would never come on Wednesday I knew that long ago.

2. Fix the run-on sentence by doing only this: Cross out one *and* then add a period and a capital.

    I bent down, and I tied my shoe and the runner took off just then, and I missed seeing the race begin.

3. In each blank, write the number of the matching clue.

    Clue 1: "It's about time" means it's about time for you to get out the plow.

    Clue 2: "It's about time" means it's about time for it to snow again.

    a. You finally got out the plow. It's about time. It snowed again! _____

    b. You finally got out the plow. It's about time it snowed again! _____

Interjections

You were getting ready to build something, and you wanted to bring a snack.

You write: I picked up my hammer and saw rats!
I forgot my cheese.

Readers think: You saw rodents!

You mean: I picked up my hammer and saw. *Rats!* I forgot my cheese.

> **THE LOGIC**
> Without clear boundaries between an interjection and sentences, the reader may get a different meaning. This usually happens when the word used as an interjection can make sense with either sentence. (One meaning of the word "rats" is a type of animal!)
>
> **THE RULE**
> An interjection may stand alone as an exclamation. Here are some examples of such forceful interjections: Well! Oh well! Darn! Ugh! Cool! Wow! Oops! Communicate your thoughts clearly by separating the interjection from the sentences around it. (Note: A mild interjection may be punctuated with a comma. See also "Comma After Introductory Words" on page 112.)
>
> - Place ending punctuation after the complete sentence before an interjection.
> - Use a capital at the beginning of the interjection.
> - Punctuate the interjection with an exclamation mark.
> - Start the next sentence with a capital letter.

PRACTICE

1. Add punctuation and capitals to make one word an interjection.

    a. I see the tower wow it's huge

    b. She snubbed me well that's rude

2. Circle **a**, **b**, or **c** to answer this question: *Are you sick?*

    (Hint: You are always honest, and you really *are* sick.)

    a. I am well! I never knew you cared.   c. I am. Well I never. Knew you cared.

    b. I am. Well! I never knew you cared.

The Language Mechanic   Run-Ons and Fragments

YOUR TURN

1. Correct each sentence. Add punctuation before or after the interjection.

   a. Rats I lost my homework.

   b. Cool I love this song.

   c. I forgot your lunch Oops.

   d. Well I was so disgusted.

2. Change each of the following as directed to make logical sentences.

   Add two capitals, a question mark, and an exclamation mark.

   a. Do we have enough soccer players great we can play a game.

   Add two periods, a capital, and an exclamation mark.

   b. They told me to bring twenty tofu dogs to the picnic I brought two dozen rats I forgot mustard.

3. In each blank, write the number of the matching clue.

   Clue 1: You punch four phone digits.

   Clue 2: You punch three phone digits.

   a. I'm calling two-five-six-oh. I have the wrong number. _____

   b. I'm calling two-five-six. Oh! I have a wrong number. _____

   Clue 1: You are surprised that he's looking.

   Clue 2: He seems healthy.

   c. He's looking well! _____

   d. He's looking. Well! _____

CHALLENGE

1. Fix the sentences as described below so they make sense. (Hint: As a verb, *darn* means to mend or repair clothing.)

   a. Add a period, a question mark, two capitals, and an exclamation mark so *darn* is an interjection.

   Will you fix my clothes I wish you would darn those holey socks show my toes.

   b. Add one punctuation mark so *darn* is a verb.

   Will you fix my clothes I wish you would darn those holey socks that show my toes.

2. Punctuate and capitalize so there are four interjections.

   Oh I dropped my ring. It's hiding under the chair. Can I reach it? Yikes a spider is on my finger. I'll try again ouch I burned my hand on the heater. Now I've got it cool.

   Explain two different ways the last five words could be understood.

   _____

   _____

   _____

   _____

Direct Quotations

Cory thinks that he looks like a dried prune.

You write: Cory says I look like a dried prune.

Readers think: You look like a dried prune.

You, the writer!

You mean: Cory says, "I look like a dried prune."

> **THE LOGIC**
>
> Leaving off the quotation marks or using them in the wrong place can tell your reader the wrong thing. Above, readers think Cory is speaking about the writer!
>
> **THE RULE**
>
> A quotation is the exact words that are spoken. Quotation marks make it clear which words are spoken: *"How do I use these wings?"* he asked. *"Put them on your arms,"* she said, *"and push this button."*
>
> When writing quotations, follow these rules:
> - Use quotation marks before and after the quotation to show what the speaker said.
> - Capitalize the first word in a quotation.
> - Use correct punctuation at the end of a quotation.
> - Use a comma to separate the speaker from the quotation.
> - If a quotation is split, put quotation marks around both parts of the quotation. Use a comma at the end of the first part and again before beginning the next part: *"I like her,"* he said, *"so I tease her."*

PRACTICE

1. One sentence tells you that Maude feels hot. Circle its letter.

   a. Maude says I feel hot.   **b.** Maude says, "I feel hot."

2. Add punctuation and capitals to correct each quotation.

   a. go away he snarled

   b. Is it time? she asked we are ready to go

   c. here she comes he said whether we like it or not

The Language Mechanic   Run-Ons and Fragments

YOUR TURN

1. Add capitals and periods where needed to fix the statements below.

   a. "let's go in when it rains," he said.

   b. "let's go in," he said, "when it rains"

2. Read the sentence and clue. Circle the best answer according to the clue.

   Sis asked, "Does Mom know you were brave getting your shot?"

   Clue: You complained a lot but had no tears when you got your shot.

   a. "She knows that I cried."   b. "She knows that!" I cried.

3. Add punctuation and capitals to make the number of quotations described.

   a. No quotations

      she said there were seven dogs

   b. One quotation

      she said, there were seven dogs

   c. Two quotations

      the new boy asked where is the lunchroom Jo said it's in the basement

   d. One split quotation

      give him an inch, she said, and he'll take a mile

4. In each blank, write the number of the matching clue. You have to think!

   Clue 1: He sounds like a hyena.

   Clue 2: She sounds like a hyena.

   a. She got up and yelled like a hyena, "He laughs!" _____

   b. She got up and yelled, "Like a hyena he laughs." _____

CHALLENGE

1. In each blank, write the number of the matching clue. (Use each clue only once.)

   Clue 1: She is yelling in her sleep.

   Clue 2: He is really calling.

   Clue 3: He is calling in a dream.

   a. In a dream, she yells, "He calls!" _____

   b. "In a dream," she yells, "he calls." _____

   c. "In a dream, she yells!" he calls. _____

2. Match each clue to the correct quotation. (Hint: The children have only a pencil.)

   Clue 1: The second part refers to a pencil.

   Clue 2: The second part refers to a toy.

   a. "I want a toy," she said, "that is fun to play with." _____

   b. "I want a toy," he said. "That isn't fun to play with." _____

3. Use punctuation and capitalization to show three different meanings for this sentence:

   I heard you cried John.

   _____

   _____

   _____

The Language Mechanic   Run-Ons and Fragments

Sentence Fragments

You are so cold that you are hopping around to warm up.

You write: We're chilled to.
                The bones. We're
                dancing to get warm.

Readers think: The bones were dancing to get warm.

You mean: We're chilled to *the* bones. We're dancing
                to get warm.

> **THE LOGIC**
>
> If you have fragments (pieces of sentences), the reader must decide which thoughts go together. They may come up with an idea that's different from yours. (They will do this especially if they make extra mistakes like taking *we're* as *were*!)
>
> **THE RULE**
>
> Write complete sentences. Do not break up a complete thought by adding extra capitals and periods where they don't belong.

PRACTICE

1. Part of each line is written as a fragment. Rewrite each line as one sentence.

   a. He had fun. Building his robot.

   _____

   b. He added a switch. To make the eyes move.

   _____

2. Circle the sentence that is written correctly and makes sense.

   a. They breathe oxygen. Through their skins they pick up small animals.

   b. They breathe oxygen through their skins. They pick up small animals.

   c. They breathe oxygen. Through their skins. They pick up small animals.

YOUR TURN

1. The following material contains sentence fragments. Cross out any unnecessary punctuation and capitals.

We had fun. At the fair. My parents drove us. In the car. Were you? And your friend there? The roller coaster went so fast that. My hat flew off!

2. Which of the following makes sense with the clue? Circle the letter. Think!

Clue: She does not eat spaghetti with a fork. She combs her hair in an unusual way.

a. She eats spaghetti. With a fork. She combs her hair.

b. She eats spaghetti. With a fork she combs her hair.

c. She eats spaghetti with a fork. She combs her hair.

3. Rewrite the following so it makes sense with the hint.

He writes letters. With a pen. He draws pictures. (Hint: He uses only pencils to draw.)

_____

CHALLENGE

1. Rewrite the sentences below as exactly two sentences. They must make sense!

We saw. The reindeer is fishing. Your favorite sport?

_____

_____

2. Cross out a period and a capital to make two complete sentences according to the hint given.

a. They designed the building. In 1955. We built it. (Hint: Though the building was designed in 1955, it was built later.)

b. They designed the building. In 1955. We built it. (Hint: The building was built in 1955, though it was designed earlier.)

UNIT REVIEW: Run-Ons and Fragments

Add periods, quotation marks, and capitals where needed to make sense. Where necessary, cross out punctuation and capitals that are not needed.

We decided. To start a school for pets who would come? Cats, dogs, and gerbils would. Attend even snakes might be welcome. What would we teach? Mrs. Jocer asked could you teach my snake to hop like a toad?" we said Of course we could. Dr. Jones asked if we could teach his cat. To slither no problem, we said. Could you teach my dog, Ms. Forster asked, to bark like a dog we said sure.

We began our work rats! The cat kept running the dog kept sitting quietly the snake kept slithering. Then something weird happened the cat and snake became friends the cat slithered. The snake tried. To copy the cat it couldn't run. it sprang up. And fell back again and again. The dog was so surprised. That it started to bark the owners came back. Dr. Jones was very happy to see his slithering cat Ms. Forster was thrilled to hear her dog bark. Mrs. Jocer saw her snake she said that's the best. Toad hopping I've ever seen!

They all said we were. Great. Teachers like us are hard to find, I guess.

The Language Mechanic　　　　　　　　　　　　　　　　　　　　　　　　　　Pronouns

3. PRONOUNS

Pronouns as Subject and Object

Your sisters are afraid of frogs.

You write:　　　　If frogs come near them run away!

Readers think:　　You should run if frogs come near them.

You mean:　　　　If frogs come near, *they* run away!

THE LOGIC

Mixing up subject and object pronouns can cause confusion as to who is doing what.

THE RULE

Use a subject pronoun to show who or what the sentence is about. Use an object pronoun to show who or what receives the verb's action. *She* gave *him* a ticket. (Not *her* gave *he* a ticket.)

Sometimes there is more than one subject or object. Two subjects: "*He* and *she* both climbed the wall." Two objects: "The owl howled at both *him* and *me*."

PRACTICE

1. Read the two sentences below.

　a. ___(subject)___ saw the slimy toad.　　**b.** The slimy toad saw ___(object)___.

Write an *S* over each personal pronoun below that could be used as the subject. Write an *O* over each pronoun that could be used as the object. The first two are done for you.

　S　O
　I　me　he　him　us　them　she　her　they　we　you

2. Circle each pronoun in the parentheses.

　a. Frank and (she, her) gave a present to George and (they, them).

　b. They send it to him, and (I, me) return it.

　c. They send it to him and (I, me). Return it.

The Language Mechanic   Pronouns

YOUR TURN

1. Circle each correct pronoun in the parentheses.

   a. Mr. Henson gave (we, us) a failing grade.

   b. (We, Us) don't think we deserved it.

   c. (He, Him) passed the other students.

   d. Did he like (they, them) better than us?

2. In each blank, write a pronoun to replace the words in the parentheses.

   Example: _They_ (Gus and Hermione) will arrive soon.

   a. _____ (Venetti and George and I) are going to be sick.

   b. The teacher just told _____ (Venetti and George) about a surprise test.

3. Circle the best pronoun to use in each blank.

   a. I hope they can lift. _____ (We, Us) are all up on the platform.

   b. I hope they can lift _____ (we, us) all up on the platform.

4. In each blank, write the number of the matching clue.

   Clue 1: You must watch the road.

   Clue 2: They watch the road.

   a. You drive him and her. Watch the road until you return. _____

   b. You drive. He and she watch the road until you return. _____

5. Cross out any incorrect pronoun and write the correct pronoun above it.

   Come with we smart people. You and us will join the mighty Wookajigs. You can see them staring at we.

The Language Mechanic   Pronouns

CHALLENGE

1. In each blank, write the number of the matching clue.

    Clue 1: Three people open the door.

    Clue 2: One person opens the door.

    a. She steadies the load while you help him and I open the door. _____

    b. She steadies the load while you help him and me open the door. _____

2. Think about the differences between these two sentences:

    I like toads better than he.   I like toads better than him.

    Sometimes words are left out because they are understood. The first sentence means *I like toads better than he does*. (In this case, *he* is the subject of the phrase *he does*.) The second sentence means *I like toads better than I like him*. (In this case, *him* is the object of the phrase *I like him*.)

    You run an obstacle course with two friends. Ahead, you see two hurdles. Explain the meaning of each of the following sentences. (Draw a picture if it helps!)

    I can jump higher than them.

    a. _____

    I can jump higher than they.

    b. _____

Possessive Pronouns

Jan wouldn't let Tameeka use Jan's ball, so Tameeka threw her own ball.

You write: Jan wouldn't share the ball, so Tameeka threw her.

Readers think: Tameeka was so upset she threw Jan.

You mean: Tameeka threw *hers*.

THE LOGIC

If you use the wrong form of a possessive pronoun, it may be read as a non-possessive pronoun. In the example above, *her* seems to be a regular pronoun.

THE RULE

Use possessive pronouns to show that something is owned, or possessed. The form of possessive pronouns depends on whether or not the noun is given: It's *my ball*. (*ball* is the noun) It's *mine*. (no noun) Use the list below to help you do the exercises.

		SINGULAR	PLURAL
(Need noun)	(Need no noun)	(Need noun)	(Need no noun)
my		mine	ourours
your	yours	your	yours
her, his, its	hers, his, its	their	theirs

PRACTICE

1. Circle the correct word to complete each sentence.

   a. Can I borrow one of (your, yours) hats?

   b. I can't find (my, mine) hat, and I'm having a bad hair day.

   c. The boys are wearing (their, theirs) baggy shorts.

   d. Let's wear (our, ours) too.

2. In each blank, write the number of the matching clue.

   Clue 1: You want to meet someone's cousin.

   Clue 2: You ask your cousin to show his car.

   a. Let me see yours, Cousin. _____

   b. Let me see your cousin. _____

YOUR TURN

1. Circle the correct pronouns.

    a. Did you see your hat move? (My, Mine) is chasing it! My hat is following (your, yours). No wonder! Your cat is under your hat. (Its, It) whiskers are sticking out!

    b. I see (yours, your) dog by my desk. That looks like (mine, my) homework he's chewing. That is (mine, my)! Why can't he chew (your, yours)?

2. In each blank, write the number of the matching clue.

    Clue 1: We ended up with the pizza.   **Clue 2:** He ended up with the pizza.

    a. We took his pizza. _____   b. We took him pizza. _____

3. Fill in the two blanks with a possessive pronoun and a noun. Fill in the single blank with a possessive pronoun. (See "The Rule" on page 27 if necessary.) Choose words that make sense!

    a. My father got to see _____ _____ after he went bald.

    b. We won the tournament because _____ _____ was the best.

    c. They thought _____ was best.

CHALLENGE

1. For sentences **a** and **b** below, decide which sentence should come next, i or ii. Write the number of the best answer in each blank.

    a. My sister and your sister love animals. _____

    b. I can't see my pet, the cat, but _____

        i. I see your pet, the dog.   ii. I see yours pet the dog.

2. In each blank, write the number of the matching clue.

    Clue 1: Trip is a verb.   **Clue 2:** Trip is a noun.

    a. Clean the floor before you trip. _____

    b. Clean the floor before your trip. _____

The Language Mechanic · Pronouns

First Person Last

You and your partner receive a trophy for winning the championship.

You write: The award was for me and you.

Readers think: You think of yourself first. Your friend is an afterthought.

You mean: The award was for *you* and *me*.

> **THE LOGIC**
>
> Placing yourself first seems rude. It sounds as if you think you are the only one of real importance. Keep your friends and other people happy by showing that you think they are important too. Treat them well, and they will do the same for you.
>
> **THE RULE**
>
> When you mention yourself and another person, place yourself (first person) last. "First person" includes *I*, *me*, *we*, and *us*.
>
> - Fred and *I* will play.
> - Mom and *we* are shopping.
> - Do it for the coach and *me*.
> - Come get them and *us*.

PRACTICE

1. Circle the letter of the sentence in which pronouns are in the correct positions.

    a. I and Sid saw a good show.

    b. Cheryl and I went to wrestle some alligators.

    c. Sadie gave me and her a dirty look.

2. Fill in the blanks using the choices in parentheses. Put the first person last!

    a. (He, I) _____ and _____ are bathing the wild cat.

    b. Dad assigned the job to _____ and _____. (me, her)

    c. (We, They) _____ and _____ are bathing the wild cat.

    d. Dad assigned the job to _____ and _____. (them, us)

The Language Mechanic   Pronouns

YOUR TURN

1. Circle the letter of each correct sentence. A sentence is correct if the pronouns are in the correct positions.

    a.   Kerry went with us and Jack.

    b.   Kerry and we went with Jack.

    c.   Kerry went with Jack and us.

2. Fill in the blanks correctly using the choices given.

    a.   (Mom, I) _____ and _____ enjoyed the play.

    b.   It was about kids like _____ and _____ (Sis, me).

    c.   Give the bread to _____ and _____ (them, us).

    d.   When are _____ and _____ going treasure hunting? (we, they)

3. Circle the correct order of pronouns to complete the sentence.

    a.   _____, _____, and _____ wanted to fly.

    John, I, Lester   I, John, Lester   John, Lester, I

    b.   They gave _____, _____, and _____ lessons.

    Rula, Cappy, me   Rula, me, Cappy   Me, Rula, Cappy

4. Circle each correct pronoun.

    Maybe they will find (us, them) and (us, them)! Maybe (we, my brother) and (we, my brother) will bury some coins. The (kids, grownups) and (kids, grownups) will find them.

CHALLENGE

1. Circle any pronouns that should be moved. Draw arrows to show where to move them.

    She, my parents, your brother, and they will arrive at noon. We and they will all look at pictures of Clarence, you, me, and Dad.

UNIT REVIEW: Pronouns

Read each paragraph. Correct any pronoun errors by crossing out the error and writing the correct word above it.

PET SWAP

Sister and I and Brother all had pets. He had a cat that her liked. I said him should give her his cat. Sister would then give hers dog to me. Then I would let he have mine raptor. I would take the monkey and gerbil from him and her. Brother would then share my mongoose with she. Me and they would be as happy as clams.

DANGER ON MARS

Gerard and me spent two days on Mars without food. Our folks had given he and I a hundred dronchoks each. It had been a rough landing in our Planet Rover. We thought the MarCats would repair the Rover. Instead, them took both his money and my. We and they were now enemies. We wanted to put distance between us and them. I and Gerard were now in danger. It looked bad for me and him. I knew others had survived they Mars journey. We would just have to live through our, too.

4. MODIFIERS

Adjectives and Adverbs

A man is sad as he paints a picture of a smiling woman.

You write: He painted her sad.

Readers think: He made the woman look sad.

You mean: He painted her *sadly*.

> **THE LOGIC**
>
> Adjectives and adverbs are used to describe other words. If you are not careful, your modifier may be describing the wrong word! *He painted her sad* means *she* looked sad. *He painted her sadly* means *he* felt sad as he painted.
>
> **RULE 1 (Adjectives)**
>
> Use an adjective to describe a noun: *yellow* cat, *scary* monster, *fuzzy* spider.
>
> **RULE 2 (Adverbs)**
>
> Use an adverb to describe a verb, an adjective, or an adverb: *quickly* ran, *dark* yellow dress, very *slowly* moved. Many adjectives can be turned into adverbs by adding *ly*.

PRACTICE 1: Adjectives

1. There is one adjective in each sentence below. Circle each adjective.

    a. When I sing, my voice is scratchy. I sound like sharp nails on a blackboard.

    b. He dug a deep hole. It was still too shallow to bury the box.

2. In each blank, write an adjective of the type shown.

    a. She was a _____ runner. (speed)

    b. His _____ ties had stripes. (color)

    c. She was wrapped in a _____ towel. (size)

    d. I was poor so I got a(n) _____ pair of shoes. (cost)

The Language Mechanic   Modifiers

PRACTICE 2: Adverbs

1. Use the underlined adjective to create an adverb to write in the blank. (Remember: many adverbs end in *ly*.)

   a. I was slow. I ran _____ to the store.

   b. I was careful. I painted the trim _____.

   c. I was light. I tiptoed _____ through the room.

   d. They were clumsy. They moved _____ over the field. (Hint: change y to i)

   e. I was a bad player. I played _____.

PRACTICE 3: Adjectives and Adverbs

1. In each blank, write the number of the matching clue.

   EXAMPLE

   Clue 1: She seemed to be a quick person.

   Clue 2: The way she came into view was quick.

   a. She appeared quick. __1__   b. She appeared quickly. __2__

   Clue 1: It took her awhile to look.

   Clue 2: We could tell she was slow.

   c. She looked slow. _____   d. She looked slowly. _____

2. Be careful how you use *good* and *well*. *Good* is an adjective: *good* job. *Well* can be an adverb: Do the job *well*. *Well* can also be an adjective: See the *well* baby. (healthy baby)

   The words in parentheses give a hint about the meaning of the statement. For each sentence, use the hint to decide what kind of modifier is in italics. Write *adjective* or *adverb* in the blank.

   a. He looks *good*. (Hint: He is handsome.)   _____

   b. He looks *well*. (Hint: He looks healthy.)   _____

   c. He sings *well*. (Hint: He can carry a tune.) _____

The Language Mechanic   Modifiers

YOUR TURN

1. Circle each correct adjective or adverb.

   a.   He (slow, slowly) raised the curtain. The curtain was very (slow, slowly).

   b.   The (sad, sadly) woman wept. She wept (sad, sadly) into her soup.

2. In each blank, write the number of the matching clue.

   Clue 1: He looks in all directions.   **Clue 2:** He appears to be gentle.

   a.   He looks careful. _____   b.   He looks carefully. _____

   Clue 1: He feared he would miss something.

   Clue 2: He appeared to be fast.

   c.   He looked quickly. _____   d.   He looked quick. _____

3. Circle each correct adjective or adverb.

   a.   The road workers had a machine to flatten the road. They rolled the road (smooth, smoothly). (Hint: Think how the road ended up.)

   b.   It was rough rolling our bikes over the trail. We rolled over the road (rough, roughly). (Hint: Think how they rolled their bikes.)

4. In each blank, write the number of the matching clue.

   Clue 1: She built her car to be the fastest.

   Clue 2: She didn't take long to build her car.

   a.   She made her car quickly. _____   b.   She made her car quick. _____

The Language Mechanic   Modifiers

CHALLENGE

1. Match each clue to the statement it describes.

   Clue 1: The light bulb wasn't fake.   **Clue 2:** The bulb was not heavy.

   a. It was a real light bulb. _____   b. It was a really light bulb. _____

2. For each statement, explain the meaning. The first one has been done for you.

   a. She smells well.   _Her nose works correctly._

   b. He smells good.   _____

   c. They look well.   _____

Comparative/Superlative Modifiers

You describe a fight between the alien and the human, Chocko.

You write: Chocko kicks with his strongest leg.

Readers think: Chocko is an alien who has more than two legs.

You mean: Chocko kicks with his *stronger* leg.

> **THE LOGIC**
>
> Using the wrong form of modifier suggests a different number of things being compared. (Above, *strongest* suggests Chocko has three or more legs!)
>
> **THE RULE**
>
> Use the comparative form to compare two things (one is *bigger* than the other). Use the superlative form of modifier to show how one stands out from two or more others (one is biggest of all).
>
> - To make regular comparative or superlative forms, start with the positive form and add *er* or *est:* mad, madder, maddest.
> - If the positive form has several syllables, use *more* or *most* with the positive form: *more* beautiful, *most* beautiful.
> - Irregular comparative or superlative forms have to be memorized: *badly, worse, worst* (adverbs); *good, better, best* (adjectives).

PRACTICE

1. Circle the word in parentheses that makes the best sense.

    a. We each have (some, more, most) money. Of the two of us, I have (some, more, most). Of the whole class, Ira has (some, more, most).

    b. Bob, Sam, and Harry chase Mary and Dan. She is the (more fast, faster, fastest) of all.

    c. Bob, Sam, and Harry chase Mary and Dan. She is the (faster, more fast, fastest) of the two.

The Language Mechanic																																		Modifiers

YOUR TURN

1. Circle the correct word for each blank according to the clue.

   a. My parents are both tall, but Mom is the (taller, tallest) of them.

   b. Mom is the (taller, tallest) of my four foster parents.

2. Circle the correct form of *good* or *bad.*

   a. Of all the desserts, my cake looked the (worse, worst) but tasted (better, best).

   b. Hap's dessert was pretty. My sundae looked worse but tasted (better, best).

3. Circle the correct word for each blank.

   a. Jeri had $10. Bertha had $20, so she had _____ (more, the most, the least). Clarita had $30, so she had _____ (more, the most, the least).

   b. I had _____ (little, less, least) money than they did.

   c. Plucky writes with her _____ (stronger, strongest) hand.

   d. Kerry was the _____ (livelier, liveliest) pony of all the ones in the herd.

CHALLENGE

1. Circle the best description according to the clue.

   Clue: The bear is chasing the two of us.

   a. The faster of us (two, three) will escape.

   b. The fastest of us (two, three) will probably smack his lips.

   Clue: He always showed up and did his work.

   c. He was (more dependable, dependablest, most dependable) of all the kids.

   d. He was even (dependabler, more dependable, most dependable) than Judy.

2. For each clue, circle the letter of the true sentence.

   Clue: I am the smarter of the students.

   a. There are only two students.   b. There are more than two students.

   Clue: I am the slowest of us kids.

   c. There are only two kids.   d. There are more than two kids.

Articles: A, An

You were stopped for speeding. The officer said you would pay a fine.

You write: When I asked, "How was my speed?" the officer said, "That's fine."

Readers think: The officer didn't give you a ticket.

You mean: The officer said, "That's *a* fine."

> **THE LOGIC**
> If a singular noun has no article or other modifier in front of it, the noun seems to be a modifier. In "That's fine," *fine* is an adjective.
>
> **THE RULE**
> Use articles *a* and *an* before a singular noun (*an* elephant, *a* horse) or noun phrase (*a* beautiful sky, *an* elegant gown).

PRACTICE

1. Cross out each sentence that is not written correctly.

   a. Give me chair.

   b. Give me a chair.

   c. I hear an elephant trumpeting.

   d. I hear an elephants trumpeting their sounds.

2. In each blank, write the number of the clue that matches the statement.

   Clue 1: I'm building well.

   Clue 2: I'm building a well.

   a. You are very good at building. _____

   b. You are making a place to get water. _____

The Language Mechanic   Modifiers

YOUR TURN

1. Cross out each sentence that is NOT written correctly.

   a. She is a beautiful girl.   d. I have wood table.
   b. She is beautiful girl.   e. I have a wood table.
   c. They are a beautiful girls.   f. I have wood tables.

2. Circle the word that goes in the blank.

   a. Something is wrong in here. It smells _____. (fishy, a fishy, fish, a fish)
   b. The dog is acting excited. It smells _____ (bird, a bird).

3. In each blank, write the number of the clue that best answers the question.

   Clue 1: I'm taking sculpture.   **Clue 2:** I'm taking a sculpture.

   a. What class will you take? _____   b. What art piece will you buy? _____

   Clue 1: Where is he going?   **Clue 2:** What is he going to do?

   c. He is going to a race.   d. He is going to race.

CHALLENGE

1. In each blank, write the number of the matching clue.

   Clue 1: He's learning construction.   **Clue 2:** He's looking for a way inside.

   a. He's studying building. _____   b. He's studying a building. _____

   Clue 1: You see him through a field of grass stalks.
   Clue 2: You look at him through a small tube.

   c. You see him through straw. _____ d. You see him through a straw. _____

2. In each blank, write the number of the clue that answers the question.

   Clue 1: I'm going on a fast.   **Clue 2:** I'm going on fast.

   a. How are you entering the highway? _____
   b. What's new with your diet? _____

Articles: A and The With General & Specific Nouns

Most dogs weigh less than 10 pounds. This one weighs 200 pounds.

You write: A dog weighs 200 pounds.

Readers think: Most dogs weigh 200 pounds!

You mean: *The* dog weighs 200 pounds.

> **THE LOGIC**
>
> If you use *a* instead of *the* before a noun, the reader thinks you mean *any* of that noun, not a particular one. Above, using *a* suggests any dog weighs 200 pounds.
>
> **THE RULE**
>
> The words *a* and *an* are indefinite articles. Use *a* and *an* before a noun when you don't mean a definite one (I got *a* chair). The word *the* is a definite article. Use *the* before a noun when you mean a definite one (I got *the* chair). If there is only one of the noun, use *the*: From outer space, he saw *the* Earth. (not *an* Earth)
> (**Note:** Also see use of *a* or *an* on page 38.)

PRACTICE

1. Circle the correct word in each statement. Use the clue to help you.

  Clue: Fluffy has given birth to four kittens.

  a. (A, The) mother is feeding her kittens.

  b. (A, The) kitten has climbed over the rest.

2. In each blank, write the number of the question you would ask.

  1. How big is a newborn baby?
  2. How big is the newborn baby?

  a. Your neighbor just gave birth to a son. _____

  b. You are helping your friend study human growth. _____

The Language Mechanic   Modifiers

YOUR TURN

1. Write *a* or *the* in each blank (*a* for general, *the* for specific).

   I brought my chair, my sunglasses, and two books. _____ book about rockets is lighter than _____ laptop computer. It is heavier than _____ sunglasses I brought.

2. In each blank, write *a* or *the* according to the clue.

   Clue: There are four blue eggs and one pink egg.

   a. "Give me _____ blue egg."   b. "Give me _____ pink egg."

3. Circle the word that makes sense in each sentence according to the hint.

   a. Don't look directly at (a, the) moon. (Hint: We have only one moon.)

   b. We saw (a, the) moon of Jupiter. (Hint: Jupiter has 16 moons.)

4. In each blank, write the number of the matching clue.

   Clue 1: The teacher is taking your pen because you've been misusing it.

   Clue 2 The teacher has nothing to write with.

   a. He says, "Give me the pen." _____   b. He says, "Give me a pen." _____

CHALLENGE

1. In each set of parentheses, circle *A* or *The*.

   Clue: Of the five bubbles, three are medium-sized.

   (The, A) biggest bubble is about to pop! (The, A) medium-sized one is floating past me. Another goes out the door. (The, A) last medium-sized bubble splatters on the floor. (The, A) smallest bubble floats down and rests on my hand.

2. In each blank, write the number of the matching clue.

   Clue 1: The dog is limping.   **Clue 2:** The woman is limping.

   a. She broke a left foot. _____   b. She broke the left foot. _____

3. Circle the true statement. (Hint: He picked a blue dress.)

   a. There were more than one blue dress.   b. There was one blue dress.

Misplaced Modifiers

The girl was running as she caught the ball.

You write: The girl caught the ball running.

Readers think: The ball was caught as it ran!

You mean: The running girl caught the ball.

THE LOGIC

A modifier tells about the word it is close to. If you put the modifier in the wrong place, readers think it describes another word.

THE RULE

Place a modifier next to the word you want it to modify. Modifiers can be adjectives, adverbs, adjective phrases, or adverb phrases.

PRACTICE

1. Cross out the two incorrect statements.

   Clue: The man is the one dancing.

   a. The man catches his sweater dancing on a nail.

   b. The dancing man catches his sweater on a nail.

   c. The man catches his dancing sweater on a nail.

   d. The man dancing catches his sweater on a nail.

2. In each blank, write the number of the matching clue.

   Clue 1: The dog wears the bikini.

   Clue 2: The girl wears the bikini.

   a. The girl sits by the dog in the bikini. _____

   b. The girl in the bikini sits by the dog. _____

   c. In the bikini, the girl sits by the dog. _____

The Language Mechanic   Modifiers

YOUR TURN

1. Under each clue, cross out the sentence that is incorrect.

   Clue: The man is the one laughing.

   a. The man saw the cows laughing.

   b. The laughing man saw the cows.

   c. The man laughing saw the cows.

   Clue: The thinking was done seriously.

   d. The boy thought about training the dog seriously.

   e. The boy thought seriously about training the dog.

   f. The boy seriously thought about training the dog.

2. In each blank, write the number of the matching clue.

   Clue 1: The man is waving his arms.

   Clue 2: The cat has arms and is waving them.

   a. The man chased the cat waving his arms. _____

   b. The man waving his arms chased the cat. _____

   Clue 1: The animal was jumping.

   Clue 2: The girl was jumping.

   c. The girl was scaring the elephant jumping up and down. _____

   d. The girl jumping up and down was scaring the elephant. _____

3. For each statement, draw an arrow to show where the underlined modifier should go. The first has been done for you.

   a. My hair needs to be cut <u>badly.</u> (Hint: You don't really want it to *look* bad.)

   b. The girl held up the toad <u>giving her speech</u>. (Hint: The toad didn't speak.)

   c. The people watched the reindeer <u>throwing snowballs</u>.
      (Hint: The reindeer were not throwing anything.)

The Language Mechanic	Modifiers

CHALLENGE

1. After each statement, tell who is smacking their lips.

   a. The boys looked at the hungry bunnies smacking their lips. _____

   b. Smacking their lips, the boys looked at the chocolate bunnies. _____

2. Fill each blank with a given adjective or adverb to make the best sense. (Hint: Adverbs describe verbs.)

   Adjectives: hopping, small   Adverb: quickly

   a. The _____ bunny _____ chased the _____ butterfly.

   Adjectives: spotted, tall   Adverb: slowly

   b. A _____ snake _____ slithers in the _____ grass.

UNIT REVIEW: Modifiers

Cross out any incorrect words and write the correct word above it. Circle any misplaced words and draw an arrow to its correct place.

Example: The boy steps on a frog (dancing). He dances ~~good~~ well.

1. I was excitedly about leaving San Jose! There were two flights to Ottawa. I would take the earliest one then change planes in Chicago. That's why I got up at 5:00 A.M. A boy can't catch an early plane sleeping!

2. The flight would take off large at 6:00. A sign said the flight would be late! I would have to wait a hour longer. I ate a egg. I read a comic book. At 6:45, we boarded the plane. At last! I quick fastened my long seatbelt so it was tightly.

3. The pilot said Chicago had snowstorms. We would have to wait another whole hour to go! It seemed like the longer hour in my life. What would I do? I had one game and two books. I played an only game I had. I read the book. Later, I'd read the other one. My right hand was sore, so I held the book with my weakest hand.

4. Finally, we took off. A airplane can fly very smooth. This was an smooth flight at first. Then it got roughly. I looked at the couple in the next seat. The man missed the excitement snoring. The woman tried to watch the movie shaking. She was the most nervous of those two.

5. After awhile, the weather got gooder. The sun shone more bright than before. The clouds were whitest than ever. I was the more happier of all passengers.

5. VERBS

Past, Present, and Future Tense

Your friends weigh a lot. They had a lot of milk when they were babies.

If you write: They weigh 85 pounds because they drink a lot of milk as babies.

Readers think: You know babies that weigh 85 pounds now!

You mean: They weigh 85 pounds because they *drank* a lot of milk as babies.

THE LOGIC

Using the wrong verb form may give the wrong message about the time of an action.

THE RULE

Verb tense is used to show when an action happens. Use the correct tense for regular verbs, as shown below. (Irregular verb tenses are shown on pages 47–48.)

- **Present Tense**—For actions happening now, use the plain verb (but add *s* to the third person singular): *I ask, you ask, she/he asks, we ask, you ask, they ask*
- **Past Tense**—For actions that happened before now, add *ed* to the plain verb: *I asked, you asked, she/he asked, we asked, you asked, they asked*
- **Future Tense**—For actions that will happen later, add *will* in front of the plain verb: *I will ask, you will ask, she/he will ask, we will ask, they will ask*

PRACTICE

1. Circle each correct tense of the verb so that all the statements make sense. Use each tense only once.

    Yesterday I (will learn, learned, learn) a lot. Today I (will learn, learned, learn) even more. Tomorrow I (will learn, learned, learn) the most.

2. Number the three actions in the order they happen in the sentences below.

    We will eat soon. We hoped to see a movie. Now we wait.

    eat ____   wait ____   hope ____

The Language Mechanic   Verbs

YOUR TURN

1. In each sentence, circle the correct tense of the verb given. (The first is done.)

   a. The band (played, play, (will play)) next Thursday.

   b. We will ride tomorrow. I'm sure we (will enjoy, enjoy) it.

   c. I already (will play, play, played) the best I could.

   d. I couldn't hear her when she (whispers, whispered, will whisper) in my ear.

   e. Give me some time. Then I (finished, will finish) my story.

   f. He looked like Dad when he was young. Now he (looks, looked) like Mom.

2. In each blank, write a different tense of the given verb. Use each of the 3 tenses (past, present, future). Don't use the same tense twice.

   I want to know what time you _____ (open) my gift. I don't want to miss it! I _____ (miss) it last time. I was very unhappy. Oh, I see you are doing it now. Your are smiling as you _____ (untie) the ribbon. I know you'll be surprised.

CHALLENGE

1. In each blank, give the tense of the underlined verb. Write **P** for past, **Pr** for present, and **F** for future.

   People <u>gaze</u> into special screens. ___ The screens are hooked up to smart machines. Earlier screens <u>showed</u> only two colors. ___ Now they have lots of color. Pictures <u>move</u> around like they do on TV! ___ Maybe the pictures <u>will look</u> even more real in a few years. ___ Maybe even the monitors themselves <u>will change</u>. ___ Before, pictures <u>appeared</u> on a flat screen. ___ Maybe they will soon appear out of thin air!

The Language Mechanic · Verbs

Irregular Verb Forms

You and your friends completed the entire songbook.

If you write: We singed everything in our songbook.

Readers think: You burned your songbooks!

You mean: We *sang* everything in our songbook.

THE LOGIC

Treating irregular verbs like regular ones can cause problems. You may be using a word that is different from what you mean.

THE RULE

Use the correct tense form for irregular verbs.

- Present and past tenses: Use the irregular verb chart on page 49 to help you do the exercises.
- Future tense: Put *will* before the plain verb: I *will go*.

PRACTICE

1. Underline each correct tense in parentheses.

    Right now, I (take, took) piano lessons. Last year I (take, taked, took) sky diving lessons. Next year I (will take, take, will took) piano lessons while sky diving.

2. In each blank, write the number of the matching clue.

    Clue 1: I do my planting now.   **Clue 2:** I had a nice sight.

    Clue 3: I did cut some wood.   **Clue 4:** I look at a tall plant.

    a. I seed a lovely garden. _____   c. I see a tree. _____

    b. I sawed a tree. _____   d. I saw a lovely garden. _____

IRREGULAR VERBS

Be careful with these verbs. They do not form the past tense in the same way that regular verbs do.

Present	Past	Present	Past
bring	brought	ride	rode
catch	caught	ring	rang
come	came	rise	rose
do	did	run	ran
draw	drew	say	said
drive	drove	see	saw
eat	ate	set	set
fall	fell	shake	shook
fly	flew	sing	sang
get	got	sink	sank
give	gave	sit	sat
go	went	shine	shone
grow	grew	speak	spoke
have	had	stand	stood
hit	hit	steal	stole
is	was	swing	swung
leave	left	take	took
lie	lay	think	thought
lose	lost	throw	threw
read	read	wear	wore

The Language Mechanic   Verbs

YOUR TURN

1. Circle the word that should go in the blank.

    a. He took a drive. He _____. (drived, droven, drove)

    b. He wanted to draw, so he _____. (drawed, drewed, drew)

    c. She hates to fall. She _____ on her knee. (falled, felled, fell)

2. Cross out each word that is wrong and write the correct word above it.

    a. The dove flue down the chimney flew. (Hint: a flue is a passageway.)

    b. We road along the path as they rided on the rode.

    c. Only one branch had leaved, so we leaved to find a park with nicer trees.

    d. We readed the book as he red the paper.

    e. She doed the dishes with a handsome dude.

3. Match meanings that are similar. In each blank, write the number of the matching clue.

    Clue 1: He said what was not true.   **Clue 2:** He was resting.

    Clue 3: He is now lying down.

    a. He lied on the floor. _____   c. He lies on the floor. _____

    b. He lay on the floor. _____

CHALLENGE

1. Cross out the wrong verb form and write it correctly.

    She stealed the money to buy food. They steeled the tool to make it harder.

2. In each statement, both words work. Explain why.

    a. The two boys ate equal parts. They (halved, had) the cake.

    _____

    b. The girl (saw, sawed) a log in the woods.

    _____

Parallel Construction for Tense

You did read a book and watch the news earlier. You are not doing either now.

You write: I read a book and watch the news.

Readers think: You are reading and watching now.

You mean: I read a book and *watched* the news.

> **THE LOGIC**
>
> If you use different tenses for things that happen at the same time, your meaning may be hard to understand. The reader takes both *read* and *watch* to be present tense. (We say the tenses are parallel when they are the same tense.)
>
> **THE RULE**
>
> Use the same verb tense for all actions that happen at the same time. In this sentence, all of the verbs are in present tense: *They enter, rise, and exit.* The following sentences are confusing because the tenses are mixed.
> - Incorrect: *We sleep as we travelled.* Correct: We *sleep* as we *travel* or We *slept* as we *travelled.*
> - Incorrect: *When he arrived, he hands us toys.* Correct: When he *arrived*, he *handed* us toys, or When he *arrives*, he *hands* us toys.

PRACTICE

1. Circle the letter of the sentence that is written correctly.

    a. She gives him a hug when he said he loved her.

    b. Take your shoes off when I mopped the floor.

    c. The sun shone brightly as we worked.

2. Fix the following sentences so there is no confusion. Cross out the verb you want to change. Write the correct form in the blank.

    a. We ate pancakes and find a dime in the batter. _____

    b. Did you do your own homework, or do you copy someone? _____

The Language Mechanic — Verbs

YOUR TURN

1. Circle the correct verb form in parentheses. Be sure the statement makes sense.

> He (walked, will walk) to the costume store and (picks, picked) the best rubber nose.

2. Write the tense that makes sense. Use a form of the verb given in parentheses.

- **a.** It _____ hard to read because of yesterday's clouds. (is)
- **b.** The game was at Juan's last night. We all _____ turns pitching. (take)
- **c.** She gets so angry that her face _____ red. (turn)

3. Sometimes the present tense can be used with the future tense. That's because phrases like "when I kick" and "before you go" already carry the idea of future action, but the helping verb *will* is left off.

Circle all choices that could make sense in the blank.

- **a.** While we fly, we _____ chess. (played, will play)
- **b.** After we're done, we _____ lunch. (ate, eat, will eat)

CHALLENGE

1. Different tenses in the same sentence show that two actions take place at <u>different</u> times. Circle the letters of all sentences that make sense.

- **a.** I will take this class again because I failed it.
- **b.** Coach tells me I'm good when I played.
- **c.** I ate earlier because the kitchen closes at one today.

2. The following statements are all written correctly. Circle the letter of the one that uses parallel tenses.

- **a.** Since he practiced last night, he will do well today.
- **b.** When I find the gold, I will share it.
- **c.** I can fly the plane because I filled it with fuel.

Helping Verbs

Behind the bushes, a dog bit George.

If you write: George attacked behind the bushes.

Readers think: George is the one who did the attacking!

You mean: George *was* attacked behind the bushes.

> **THE LOGIC**
>
> If you leave out the helping verb, the meaning may be confused. In the example above, it seems that the subject did the acting (George attacked). Instead, George was acted on by something else.
>
> **THE RULE**
>
> Some verb forms need an extra verb or verbs besides the main verb. The extra verb is called the helping verb (auxiliary verb) and is placed before the main verb. Together, the helper(s) and main verb form the verb phrase. The helping verb gives the tense of the verb phrase. It must show agreement with the subject. (I *was* walking—not *were*). Forms of the following verbs are used as helping verbs: *be, have, do, can, may, will, shall, must.*

PRACTICE

1. Add one of these helping verbs in each statement so that it makes sense: *am, was, has,* and *did.*

    a. I _____ walking by myself when it happened.

    b. I _____ walking by myself again today.

    c. He _____ seen them fly.

    d. Who said I didn't go? I tell you I _____ go.

2. Circle all sentences that could agree with the clue.

    a. **Clue:** You haven't gone yet.

       1. You could go.   2. You have gone.   3. You will go.

    b. **Clue:** She is finished planning.

       1. She is planning.   2. She does plan.   3. She did plan.

The Language Mechanic   Verbs

YOUR TURN

1. In each blank, write the best helping word: *were, will, must,* or *have.*

   a.   It must _____ been a cold day. They _____ shivering.

   b.   You _____ tie your shoe before you trip. I _____ not help you if you fall!

2. In each blank, write the best helping word: *did, should, are,* or *was.*

   a.   Mr. Turnig _____ driving by, so we _____ get a ride.

   b.   They _____ being lazy. They _____ be painting the wall.

3. Write each helping verb where it belongs: *am, could, should,* and *has.* The first is done for you.

         has
   He^seen the new books. He not read them without his glasses.

   I going to the race tomorrow. Maybe I get some sleep.

4. In each blank, write the number of the best answer. (Use each answer once.)

   1. I saw it.   **2.** I did see it.

   a. Who saw the report? ____   **b.** Weren't you supposed to see the movie? ____

5. Write the correct word in each blank: *have, had, will,* and *can.*

   a.   We _____ plan a trip if we _____ find the map.

   b.   We would _____ been late if we _____ not gotten a ride.

CHALLENGE

1. Add punctuation to help show the meaning of each sentence.

   a.   How far we run ___   **b.**   How far can we run ___

2. Tell how the helping verb changes the meaning of each sentence.

   a.   I painted. I am painted. _____

   b.   We run on the beach. We will run on the beach.

   _____

Linking Verbs

Your neighbors never look dirty.

If you write: The Smiths always clean.

Readers think: They keep busy scrubbing things.

You mean: The Smiths always *look* clean.

> **THE LOGIC**
> If you leave off the linking verb, the next word may look like an action verb. With the linking verb *look*, clean is an adjective describing the Smiths.
>
> **THE RULE**
> A linking verb joins the subject to another word or words: Bob *is* lazy, Joy seems tired. The other words (*lazy, tired*) describe the subject.
> Linking verbs: *am, look, seem, appear, be, become, grow, remain, smell, sound, stay, taste, feel*
> **Note:** Some linking verbs can also be used as action verbs. How can you tell whether it is a linking verb or an action verb? If it is a linking verb, a form of *be* or *seem* will make sense in its place. It will also be followed by a word that describes the subject.
> He *sounds* angry. (*seems* angry, *is* angry—linking verb)
> He *sounds* the bell. (makes it sound—action verb)

PRACTICE

1. Use the linking verb that makes sense in each blank: *look, are,* and *taste.*

    a. Anchovies _____ salty.

    b. The dogs _____ thin.

    c. They _____ kind.

2. Underline only the verbs that are used as linking verbs.

    a. Does Jon look for food? Does Jon look hungry? (Hint: *hungry* is an adjective that describes Jon.)

    b. Barb has grown sad. Her sister has grown up and left home. (Hint: Which verb is followed by a word that describes the subject?)

The Language Mechanic Verbs

YOUR TURN

1. In each blank, write a linking verb that makes sense. Choose from these linking verbs: *looked, felt,* and *smelled.*

We went to the party. The people _____ neat and clean. The food _____ delicious. Someone put a blindfold on me. I _____ a stick in my hand.

2. Write each linking verb where it makes the best sense: *sounded, grew,* and *tasted.*

Example: He ˄ full. (was)

I whacked the piñata. It full. I kept hitting it. I tired, but it finally broke! We ate all the candy. It very sweet.

3. Underline the linking verbs in each sentence.

We are happy campers. Our campsite looks pleasant. The fires seem to glow. We go to bed when we grow tired. We rise when the morning bell is loud.

CHALLENGE

1. Decide whether the underlined word is an action verb or a linking verb. Write an **L** for linking or **A** for action in each blank.

a. The boy <u>feels</u> a frog in his shirt. _____
The girl <u>feels</u> happy to be here. _____

b. The cracker <u>tastes</u> stale. _____
Jon <u>tastes</u> stale doughnuts. _____

c. We were busy all morning, and we <u>remain</u> busy now. _____
Others will leave, but we will <u>remain</u> here. _____

The Language Mechanic   Verbs

UNIT REVIEW: Verbs

Cross out any incorrect verb form. Write the correct verb form above the words. The first sentence is correct.

A   Elena was new. My friends and I make fun as she walked into the classroom. Her hair was a stringy mess that covered her eyes. Her shoes were two sizes too big, and they are scuffed. Her socks didn't even match! How could she be so careless? When Dory said, "Hi, Rags," we laugh out loud. I know Elena heared us, but I can't help it. Anyway, she deserves it. She could have paid more attention to her clothes. When she passed us, she even smells bad. She hanged her head down. She bumped into a desk and run off. Couldn't she even watch where she was going? I forgetted about her until that night.

B   The phone rang after dinner. Mom talks with her best friend, Alice, for awhile. Then Mom sayed, "No problem. She can stay here in Marcy's room." She hanged up and said, "Alice's relatives losed their house in a fire. They stayed with Alice last night, but it was crowded. The kids have no decent clothes. Alice will find them some tomorrow. Maybe you could loan the girl some of your things, Marcy. She will be over in a few minutes." I feeled sorry for the girl, but I was not ready for what I saw at the door. My mouth falled open. All I can say was "You?" It was Elena! She acts as surprised as I.

C   Suddenly, I felt ashamed. No wonder she weared shoes that were too big. No wonder she had no time or help to fix her hair. How would I feel if I have to go to school like that?

D   "I didn't know about your house, Elena. I was mean and I'm sorry," I apologized. It taked her awhile to trust me. I loaned her some nice clothes and maked her feel at home. She turned out to be really fun! I decided to introduce her to my friends. I sweared I would never make fun of anyone again. There may always be a hidden reason for the things people do.

6. AGREEMENT

Pronoun/Antecedent Agree in Gender

We looked for Mom and our dog, Jake.

You write: We found her sniffing around in the bushes.

Readers think: Mom was sniffing around in the bushes!

You mean: We found *him* sniffing around in the bushes.

THE LOGIC

Using a pronoun of the wrong gender makes it sound like you're talking about someone else.

THE RULE

A pronoun and the noun it replaces (antecedent) should agree in gender. If the noun means a female, then the pronoun should be female. If the noun means a male, the pronoun should be male. Possessive pronouns should also agree with their noun in gender.

- I lost Dad, but I found *him*.
- *John* saw *his* teacher.
- *Sally* gave us *her* books.
- *Mr. Gallowaggie* rolled *his* paper into a tube.

PRACTICE

1. Write the pronoun that makes sense.

    a. After Mom and Dad went to the hospital, _____ had a baby. (she, he)

2. Underline the pronoun in parentheses that makes sense with the clue.

    Clue: John plays bagpipes in Scottish costume. Sherry runs the sack race in slacks.

    a. (He, She) was wearing a plaid skirt.

    b. (He, She) was wearing pants.

YOUR TURN

1. Circle the correct pronoun for each choice.

   a. Jon gives Bess his lunch because (he, she) is not hungry.

   b. Bess gives it back to Jon. (She, He) is not hungry, either.

   c. Jake tells Patty (he, she) likes her hair.

   d. Dad likes to look in the mirror. Mom told Dad that (he, she) is stuck up.

2. Write the pronouns that make sense with the hint

   a. Jake is bringing his ten-year-old sister. (He, She) _____ is very excited.
      (Hint: Jake is always calm.)

   b. (She, He) _____ ran toward the bullfighter when (he, she) waved a flag.
      (Hint: The bullfighter is a woman. The bull is male.)

3. In each blank, write the number of the clue that matches each statement. (The clue gives the antecedent for the underlined pronoun.)

   Clue 1: Dr. Bill Jones was holding the baby as the mother smiled.

   Clue 2: When the boy was born, the mother smiled.

   a. The mother was happy that he had the baby. _____

   b. The mother was happy that she had the baby. _____

The Language Mechanic   Agreement

CHALLENGE

1. Make the pronouns agree with their antecedents. Cross out each incorrect pronoun and write the correct one.

   a. **Clue:** An ewe is a female sheep, and a ram is a male.

   The ewe found a field of green grass. He ran and told the ram. She was glad to hear her news.

   b. **Clue:** Donald has a dark green SUV, a large four-wheeled vehicle. Margaret has a red motorcycle (they call it a bike).

   He told her to load his bike into his SUV. He would drive him and his bike to the lake. Then he would help her unload.

   He would speed through the mountain roads on his two wheels. Meanwhile, she would stay at the lake in her dark vehicle.

2. Circle the correct pronoun in parentheses.

   Valerie owned Jonny, the male cat. Bob owned Sylvia, the female dog. When they got (his, her) cat ready to go to the vet, (his, her) dog got upset. (He, She) wanted to go, too. Mom drove them both in (his, her) new car. When (she, he) took Jonny in to get (his, her) shot, Sylvia went with her. As soon as they entered the office, Sylvia changed (his, her) mind. (He, She) no longer wanted to be there. Jonny was a brave cat. (He, She) had done this many times. (He, She) sat waiting patiently while the dog struggled to get off (his, her) leash and out the door.

Pronoun/Antecedent Agree in Number

The dog runs as it chews on some bones.

You write: The dog chewed the bones as they ran away.

Readers think: The bones were running!

You mean: The dog chewed the bones as *it* ran away.

> **THE LOGIC**
>
> Sometimes more than one noun is mentioned. If you use the wrong pronoun, the reader may think you mean a different noun. In the example, *they* seems to mean *bones* since both words are plural.
>
> **THE RULE**
>
> Make a pronoun and its noun agree "in number." For example, if the noun means just *one* person, place, or thing, use a singular pronoun. If the noun means *more than one*, use a plural pronoun. "I saw two girls. I spoke to them." (*them* agrees with *girls* because they are both plural.)

PRACTICE

1. Circle the correct words to complete each sentence. Use logic and your knowledge of noun/pronoun agreement.

   a. The rat king was squeaky clean. He blew (his, their) nose whenever (it, they) ran.

   b. He caught the other rats whenever (it, they) ran.

2. Circle the correct words to complete each sentence. Use logic and your knowledge of noun/pronoun agreement.

   a. The sun rose over the mountains. (It was, They were) like a green monster with many humps.

   b. The sun rose over the mountains. (It was, They were) like a giant lamp beaming at us.

The Language Mechanic   Agreement

YOUR TURN

1. Circle each correct pronoun or pronoun and verb choice.

    a. He bought those socks because (he was, they were) cute.

    b. She wrapped the fish with papers because (they, it) smelled bad.

    c. The clouds were over the field when (it was, they were) mowed.

    d. The clouds were over the field when (it was, they were) puffy and white.

2. Choose from these words to fill in the blanks (use each word once): *their, his, its,* and *her.*

    a. Bob did _____ homework.

    b. Betty passed _____ test.

    c. Jan and Terri took _____ turn after us.

    d. The stuffed tiger shed _____ fur.

3. Underline the correct pronoun. Make the sentences logical.

    a. The children were asleep in the car. The parents finally woke (her, him, it, them).

    b. The roller coaster queen had many secrets. She gave (it, them) to us for a nickel.

4. Underline the correct pronoun. Make the sentences logical.

    a. One night, John made soup. That night, John ate (his, their) soup.

    b. Jerry had no food of his own. After the women left, Jerry ate (his, their) soup.

CHALLENGE

1. Write a pronoun in the blank. Be sure it makes sense with the sentence!

    a. She pounded her feet on the track. _____ got very sore.

    b. The paint was too thin. Sue put it on two walls, but _____ ran.

2. Cross out any incorrect noun or pronoun. Write the correct word above.

    Several objects glided through space. First was a slender steel spoon. Behind them was a green and purple stuffed snake. A rubber duck followed. It were all moving toward a strange planet. This planet sucked all the objects from space. They was like a vacuum cleaner for the objects. It stuck to the planet like tape.

Noun or Pronoun/Verb Agree in Number

Two deer leave the herd and slide down a hillside.

You write: The deer slides down the hill.

Readers think: Only one deer slides.

You mean: The deer *slide* down the hill.

> **THE LOGIC**
>
> The singular and plural of some nouns are spelled the same (deer, fish, sheep). The verb gives the number of the noun, telling whether it is only one or more than one. Sometimes the verb is the reader's only clue to the number of the noun.
>
> **THE RULE**
>
> Make the verb agree in number with its noun or pronoun. Use a singular verb with a singular noun or pronoun: *One deer slides*. Use a plural verb with a plural noun or pronoun: *Two deer slide*. (Oddly enough, a regular singular verb for *he* or *she* ends in *s*.)
>
> - The words *this, that, these*, and *those* sometimes stand alone as pronouns (called demonstrative pronouns). They must agree with the verb. Examples: *This is* fun. *These are* fun. *Those are* fun.
> - A title stands for one work of art and is a singular subject. Example: *The painting "Dolphins" is lovely*.

PRACTICE

1. Circle the correct word in parentheses to complete each sentence. Use logic and your knowledge of noun/verb agreement.

   a. The purple and orange cat (leap, leaps) over the house!

   b. The purple and orange crayons (lie, lies) on the table.

2. Find each pronoun that disagrees with its verb. Cross it out, and write the corrected word above it.

   We has chocolate kisses. You have jelly beans. This are better than those.

The Language Mechanic   Agreement

YOUR TURN

1. Circle the correct choice in parentheses. Each noun or pronoun should agree with its verb.

   a. The parrots (is, are) talking more like the monkey.

   b. (They, It) improve their speech every day.

   c. I think that (look, looks) like a plastic nose.

   d. (Mr. Hensley and Ms. White, Ms. Ru) are teaching.

   e. It is a busy day for you and Jack. (You, He) is working at home then leaving for Mars.

2. Circle the correct verb for each noun.

   a. John (find, finds)
   b. the boys (go, goes)
   c. my uncles (drive, drives)
   d. women (rent, rents)
   e. one deer (run, runs)
   f. Sally (look, looks)
   g. mother (laugh, laughs)
   h. sisters (have, has)
   i. woman (walk, walks)
   j. several deer (eat, eats)

3. Write the correct present tense form of the given verb in each blank. Make it agree with its subject.

   a. The boy _____ (do) his work.
   b. Five deer _____ (run) down.
   c. The fifth deer _____ (leap) a bush.
   d. Those guys _____ (swim) quickly.
   e. That one _____ (eat) worms.

The Language Mechanic   Agreement

CHALLENGE

1. Now you have to think more. Read the clue then fill each blank with the pronoun or verb that makes sense.

   Clue: Only one sheep likes junk food. The rest of the flock do not. The others all like only sheep food.

   a. The sheep _____ (is, are) eating grass. Give _____ (it, them) some more.

   b. The sheep _____ (is, are) eating candy. Now I see _____ (it, them) looking for gummy worms.

2. Fill in each blank with the correct verb form: *is* or *are*.

   "Garage Sale" _____ a fun poem, but I think "The Saleswomen"

   _____ boring.

   Three monkeys _____ cute when they play, but "Three Monkeys"

   _____ scary when you see it at the theater.

3. Underline any incorrect noun or verb. Write the correct word above it.

   The pirates of third grade looks fierce. Tam and Mark look tough. He both wear eye patches. Two of the girls has parrots on their shoulders. The parrots sing, and it squawk loudly. Do not be afraid. These kids are good pirates. They help kids who are being picked on. The pirates yell at the bullies and chase him away.

The Language Mechanic   Agreement

Adjective/Noun Agree in Number

You are telling which fish is not poisonous.

You write: Only these fish should be eaten.

Readers think: It's okay to eat several of the fish.

You mean: Only *this* fish should be eaten.

> **THE LOGIC**
> Many adjectives can be used with both singular and plural nouns. Example: A red rose, red apples. In this lesson, we will use adjectives that are either singular or plural and must agree in number with their noun (one, some, all, this, these).
>
> **THE RULE**
> Use a singular adjective with a singular noun. Example: I think *one candy* is enough. Use a plural adjective with a plural noun. Example: Eating *many candies* will make you sick.

PRACTICE

1. Draw lines to match each adjective to the noun with which it agrees.

    a. some   bats   b. this   game   c. that   dresses

        one   glove   these   parks   those   necklace

2. Write *this* or *these* in each blank to make the sentence correct.

    a. I want _____ flowers to go in _____ vase.

3. Write *that* or *those* in each blank to make the sentence correct.

    a. Put _____ candies in _____ dish.

The Language Mechanic   Agreement

YOUR TURN

1. Choose the correct word and write it in the blank.

   a. I've never seen _____ (a, any) black flowers, but I once saw _____ (a, some) purple roses.

   b. If _____ (all, one) person gets to go, _____ people should go. (all, one)

   c. _____ lonely sock has no mate, but _____ socks are happily paired. (These, This, these, this)

   d. I think _____ fish are tasty, but _____ one is not. (these, this)

2. In each row, circle each adjective that is singular or plural. Write P or S beside it to show whether it is singular or plural. The first row is done for you.

   a. (these) P   ugly   thick   (four) P   (that) S
   b. tall   one   several   quiet   eleven
   c. many   lovely   this   those   purple

CHALLENGE

1. In each blank, use an adjective that agrees with the noun.

   a. _____ deer ran. They were scared.   _____ deer ran. The dogs chased it.

   b. _____ fish jumped. We saw its scales.   _____ fish jumped. I saw them splash.

2. Each underlined adjective should agree with its noun. If it does not, cross it out and write an adjective that does agree. The first has been done for you.

   I asked ~~two~~ ^one salesman for help. He showed me <u>a</u> maps. One map showed <u>two</u> parks. One map showed only <u>several</u> park. The last map showed the <u>three</u> parks I needed to find. I said, "I'll take <u>these</u> map." Then I found all of <u>that</u> parks.

Adjectives (This, That)/Noun Agree in Space or Time

The man farther away is rich. The man next to you is poor. Robin Hood takes from the rich and gives to the poor.

You write: Robin Hood takes money from this man and gives it to that man.

Readers think: Robin Hood takes money from the poor man.

You mean: Robin Hood takes money from *that* man and gives it to *this* man.

> **THE LOGIC**
>
> If you use *this* instead of *that* or *that* instead of *this*, you could give your reader a message that is the opposite of what you mean!
>
> **THE RULE**
>
> When used with nouns, *this, that, these,* and *those* are adjectives. They describe position in space or time: *this* state, *those* countries, *these* days, *that* year. The writer should use *this* and *these* to describe near things. The writer should use *that* and *those* to describe farther things. *This rug is dirty, but that one is clean. That day was hot, but this day is cold.*

PRACTICE

1. Write *this, that, these,* or *those* in the blanks to make the sentences correct.

   a. _____ door over there leads to the hall. _____ door next to me leads nowhere.

   b. _____ cats beside me fight with _____ cats over there.

2. Fill in the blanks so they make sense with the hint.

   I think _____ man saw the robber pick _____ man's pocket. (this, that)

   (Hint: The closer man wears glasses. The farther man is blind.)

The Language Mechanic   Agreement

YOUR TURN

1. In each blank, write the adjective in parentheses that makes sense. Use the hint for help.

   a. I'll put _____ sticks in the dip and _____ sticks on the drums. (these, those) (Hint: The wooden drumsticks are near you. The pretzel sticks are not.)

   b. I know _____ days were colder than _____ are. (these, those) (Hint: Now that it's July, it is warmer than it was in June.)

2. Write the correct adjective in each blank (*blue, small, red, big*) to describe the noun given.

   Clue: Your red socks and your big cat are lying nearby. Your blue socks and the small cat are in the other room.

   a. this _____ cat   c. these _____ socks

   b. that _____ cat   d. those _____ socks

3. Fill in the blank with *this or that* according to the hint.

   a. _____ vehicle can go much faster than _____ one. (Hint: You are standing next to the station wagon. The sports car is across the road.)

   b. _____ planet is full of rocks, but _____ one has sand and water. (Hint: You see a stony planet as you stand on another planet's beach.)

4. Fill each blank with a given adjective to make the best sense.

   a. _____ month is busy. _____ month will be even busier. (This, That)

   b. _____ last ride was fun. _____ one is even more fun! (This, That)

The Language Mechanic   Agreement

CHALLENGE

1. You and Meryl each have a video. She wants to trade. You don't. Write *this* or *that* in each blank.

   a. She says: Give me _____ one and you can have _____ one.

   b. You say: No, I want _____ one. You'll have to keep _____ one.

2. You can use either *this* or *that* to describe things that are the same distance from you as long as you show exactly which one you mean. Read the clue then write *left* or *right* beside each statement to show which hand you would hold out.

   Clue: You have a quarter in your left hand, a dollar in your right.

   a. That is worth 25 cents. _____   **b.** This is worth 100 cents. _____

   c. This is worth less. _____   **d.** That is worth more. _____

3. Underline each correct adjective in parentheses.

   I found 28 red and orange gummy slugs here on the table. He found 32 gray ones there on the floor. (These, Those) slugs are more colorful than (those, these) slugs. I would rather look in (that, this) spot. I think (that, this) spot is dirtier. Put (these, those) 28 slugs in the candy dish. Put (these, those) 32 slugs in the trash. Tomorrow we will have another gummy hunt. (That, This) hunt may give us one hundred good slugs. (That, This) hunt gave us only 28 good ones.

The Language Mechanic — Agreement

UNIT REVIEW: Agreement

Edit the following paragraph. Cross out words and write new ones so that words agree in number, gender, and space or time.

We live by a beach resort. Mr. Wiggle has our surfboards over at her house. Gin and I has our snowboards at our house. This boards are for the resort in the mountains. We'll use these other boards when we go to our beach. This week, we'll go to that mountain resort because it has snow. Next week, we'll come back to these beach resort because it is great for surfing.

One time when we were skiing, Gin hit a bump, and it fell on her face. I laughed so hard we got a stomachache. I was so busy laughing, I slowly glided into a tree! Now, Gin laugh at me when she remembers that day.

We have our laughs at the beach, too. One time, Arnold picked up a board that wasn't her own. He didn't notice his mistake until a boy yelled, "Thief!" Boy, were Arnold's face red! He gave it back and said we was sorry. The two boys shook hands. Now they is friends.

7. UNNECESSARY WORDS

Double Negatives

You have spent all your money.

You write: I don't have no money!

Readers think: If you don't have no money, you must have some money.

You mean: I have *no* money.
(OR I *don't* have any money.)

> **THE LOGIC**
>
> Two negative words can cause confusion or can make a sentence positive. If you use more than one negative, the reader may misunderstand you.
>
> **THE RULE**
>
> Use only one negative word to state a negative idea. *Not, no, none*, and words with "no" such as *nobody* and *nowhere* are negative words. *Hardly* and *scarcely* are also often used to help state a negative idea. Use *any* and *ever* after hardly and scarcely. (Don't use *no, never, none*, or *don't* with hardly and scarcely.)

PRACTICE

1. Circle the letter of any statement that agrees with the clue.

   Clue: All her candy is gone.

   a. She doesn't have no candy.
   b. She doesn't have any candy.
   c. She has no candy.
   d. She hasn't no candy.

2. Circle the letter of any statement that agrees with the clue.

   Clue: He loves nobody.

   a. He doesn't love nobody.
   b. He doesn't love anybody.
   c. He loves hardly anybody.
   d. He doesn't love no one.

The Language Mechanic   Unnecessary Words

YOUR TURN

1. Circle the letters of the correct statements. (Hint: You don't want more cake.)

   a. Don't give me no more cake.   c. Give me no more cake.

   b. Don't give me any more cake.   d. Give me more cake.

2. You have no time. Circle the letter of the corrrect statement.

   a. I ain't got any time.   c. I have got some time.

   b. I haven't got no time.   d. I don't have any time.

3. Rewrite the sentences correctly in the blanks. Remember: Treat *hardly* and *scarcely* as negatives.

   a. There's hardly no rain. _____

   b. We scarcely never have fun. _____

4. Your friend feels terrible. Circle the letters of all sentences that tell how she feels.

   a. She feels no good.   c. She doesn't feel no good.

   b. She doesn't feel good.   d. She does not feel good.

CHALLENGE

A double negative is sometimes used to make a special point. Two negative words can actually make a positive statement.

1. What should Sara say? In each blank, write the number of the matching clue.

   Clue 1: Sara is too full.

   Clue 2: Sara wants pie, but Dad says "no more."

   a. Don't give me "no more" pie! _____   b. Don't give me any more pie. _____

2. Circle the *real* meaning of each underlined sentence that has a double negative.

   a. Don't not do it.   Do it.   Don't do it.

   b. There's not nobody in the room.   Somebody is in there.   The room is empty.

The Language Mechanic   Unnecessary Words

Noun or Pronoun (Not Both) As Subject

You and two friends look at the "flying fish" jumping in the river.

You write: Flying fish they are fun to watch.

Readers think: Your friends are fun to watch when they are flying fish!

You mean: Flying fish are fun to watch.

> **THE LOGIC**
>
> Using both a noun and a pronoun is misleading. Words can be misread as different parts of speech. The words *flying fish* are taken as modifiers for the pronoun *they*. (Some modifiers are given as a phrase followed by a comma: *Racing model cars, the kids get excited*. The kids get excited *while* they are racing model cars.)
>
> **THE RULE**
>
> Use the noun or the pronoun, not both, as subject.
>
> Incorrect: Pandas they are cuddly.   Correct: Pandas are cuddly. They are cuddly.

PRACTICE

1. In each blank, write the number of the clue that matches the statement.

    Clue 1: You are telling Bob something.

    Clue 2: Bob has the snake.

    Clue 3: [There is an unnecessary word!]

    a. Bob, he has the boa constrictor. _____

    b. Bob he has the boa constrictor. _____

    c. Bob has the boa constrictor. _____

2. Read the sentence below. In the blank, write the letter of the sentence that should follow it. Correct the other two sentences by crossing out one word in each.

    I used my remote control. _____

    a. The plane it flew fast.   c. The remote it flew the plane.

    b. The plane it flew was fast.

The Language Mechanic   Unnecessary Words

YOUR TURN

1. Cross out any unnecessary pronouns.

   a. The ice it is cold.   **b.** The boy he won't behave.

2. Cross out any pronoun that doesn't belong.

   a. When we ice skate, it is cold. When the ice skate it is cold, his foot it won't go in.

   b. When he dodges the swooshing Snarfo, he dives into the mud. The swooshing Snarfo he dives into the mud.

3. Cross out any unnecessary pronouns. Read carefully. Some may be tricky!

   Terrence he goes to college. The college it is beautiful. The ground it is on has a hiking trail. People they hike the trail often. Walking quickly, they hike it in an hour.

4. If a noun has already been named, its pronoun may be used instead (*she* instead of Mary). Cross out the unnecessary words in each sentence.

   Example: Mary is neat. ~~Mary~~ she always picks up after herself. (S above "she")

   a. Cindy she puts on her sneakers. Then Cindy she walks 5 miles.

   b. Rosco loves music, and Rosco's his favorite music is jazz.

CHALLENGE

In this sentence, it is the cars that run fast: <u>Racing cars run fast</u>. In the underlined sentence below, we can tell that the *cheetahs* run fast.

   Eating food, the cheetahs move slowly. <u>Racing cars, they run fast.</u>

1. Match each clue to the sentence it describes. (see Misplaced Modifiers pg. 42)

   Clue 1: Cars that pass are speeding.   **Clue 2:** As they pass cars, they speed.

   a. Passing cars, they go too fast. ____   **b.** Passing cars go too fast. ____

2. For discussion: The underlined sentence in **a** is correct as written. The underlined sentence in **b** is not correct. Explain.

   a. When they ride bikes, they are bored. <u>Riding bulls, they are happy.</u>

   b. I stay away from running bulls. <u>Running bulls they are scary.</u>

Here/There With This/That

You want someone to pick up the Robot II.

You write: Take that there Robot II.

Readers think: You want Robot II to take something over there.

You mean: Take that Robot II.

> **THE LOGIC**
>
> *Here* or *there* is an adverb, so the reader will think it tells *how* something is done (or *where* you should take something).
>
> **THE RULE**
>
> Do not use *this* with *here* or *that* with *there* to describe a noun.

PRACTICE

1. Circle the letter of the sentence that is written correctly.

    a. Move this here chair.

    b. Bring that chair over here.

    c. Take that there ticket.

2. One statement uses an unnecessary word. Cross out the statement. (Hint: In **a**, you are talking to a child.)

    a. Take that there, Child.

    b. Take that there child.

    c. Take that child over there.

The Language Mechanic   Unnecessary Words

YOUR TURN

1. Circle the letter of the sentence that makes the best sense.

   a. Give me that there pie.   c. Bring the pie here.
   b. Take this here pie.   d. Bring me that pie there.

2. Correct the following sentences by crossing out unnecessary words.

   This here tiger is huge. Those there jaws are strong. What if he runs over here? Use that there stick to scare him away. Seeing the tiger over there is better than having the tiger here. We enjoy him from this here spot.

3. Read the sentence below. In the blank, write the letter of the sentence that should follow it.

   That chocolate isn't here! _____

   a. Is that chocolate there?   b. Is that chocolate there very good?

4. Cross out the unnecessary word.

   Take that over there, Teddy. Take that there teddy bear off the carpet.

CHALLENGE

1. In each blank, write the number of the clue that matches the statement.

   Clue 1: You say who you'll dance with and where.
   Clue 2: You want to tell Doll where to dance with the broom.
   Clue 3: There is an extra word.

   a. Dance with this here, Doll. _____   c. I'll dance with Bob here. _____
   b. Dance with this here doll. _____

2. Explain how this sentence might be taken in two ways. (One way would be wrong!)

   Is this train here on time?

   _____

   _____

UNIT REVIEW: Unnecessary Words

Read each paragraph. Correct any errors by crossing out the unnecessary word. Write the correct word above if necessary.

"Nobody can't see the game from here!" wails Jenny. Jenny she is right. These here seats are too high in the stands. The players don't look no bigger than ants. Jenny and I we look for better seats. There is hardly nothing left empty. I say, "Hold this here drink. Keep this sandwich here too." Then I see that there woman at the exit. I say, "Jen, she looks like she's leaving." I run over there. I ask if she's leaving.

She says, "My son he ate too much and doesn't feel no good. We've scarcely never been to a game."

I say, "I came with my sister. We can't see from our seats. Do you mind if we use those there seats of yours?"

She says, "No, Jake and I we're not coming back. Have fun."

Cross out any unnecessary pronouns.

The day ends for the playmates. Rat he scampers home. Char she walks lazily by the river. The trees they grow so tall. Her purse it feels so heavy. Near her, people they lie on the ground. She decides to lie down too.

8. PUNCTUATION ' ? ! " "

Apostrophe: Contractions

You and your friend pass notes to decide who is going to pick up the food.

If you write: Well go get the pizza!

Readers think: You want him to get it.

You mean: *We'll* go get the pizza.

> **THE LOGIC**
>
> If a contraction goes without an apostrophe, the contraction is read as a regular word. The word *we'll* (we will) becomes *well*.
>
> **THE RULE**
>
> Use an apostrophe to show where letters are missing in a contraction. The apostrophe is a signal that letters are missing.
>
> To contract means to shorten; a contraction is a shortened form of a word. You can't make a contraction out of just any words. Many contractions are based on these words (each shown with a few examples).
>
> - *not* (don't = do not, can't = cannot, wouldn't = would not, aren't = are not)
> - *will* (I'll = I will, they'll = they will, you'll = you will)
> - *be* (he's = he is, it's = it is, we're = we are, I'm = I am, who's = who is)
> - *have* (He's = he has, you've = you have, we've = we have)

PRACTICE

1. In each blank, write the contraction for the underlined words. Use the list of contractions to help you.

   a. We <u>are not</u> at home. _____
   b. <u>I will</u> be there soon. _____
   c. <u>You have</u> got my word. _____
   d. <u>She is</u> homesick. _____
   e. They <u>cannot</u> wait. _____
   f. <u>You will</u> see us. _____

2. Circle the correct word for each sentence.

   a. They are making faces, but (we're, were) looking away.
   b. They were walking this way, but we (we're, were) looking away.

The Language Mechanic   Punctuation

YOUR TURN

1. For each sentence, circle the word that makes sense.

    a.   They gave us the map because (we've, weave) got good eyes.

    b.   They gave us the yarn to (we've, weave) into a shirt.

2. You want to tell your friends that you and your family will arrive soon. Underline the sentence that you would use.

    a.   Friends, were on the way!

    b.   Friends, we're on the way!

    c.   Friends were on the way!

3. Add apostrophes where needed.

    a.   Weve got to ask what theyd like.

    b.   Shell take the cake.

    c.   Theyre going there.

    d.   It wouldnt be fun without you.

4. In each blank, write the number of the matching clue.

    Clue 1: One car ran out of gas.

    Clue 2: All cars ran out of gas.

    a.   Our car has stopped. The car's run out of gas. _____

    b.   All the cars stop. The cars run out of gas. _____

CHALLENGE

1. For each sentence, circle the word that makes sense. (Hint: Think about what *it's* might stand for.)

    a. Now I know how a wombat survives. I see what (its, it's) eating.

    b. Now I know what a wombat looks like. I see (its, it's) painting.

2. Cross out any incorrect words. Rewrite them correctly.

    a. Their going to be happy we came.

    b. She is the one whose coming with us.

3. Read and compare the two sentences. How do their meanings differ for the underlined words?

    a. They wanted to get away from home <u>but were always there.</u>

    They never go to Friday parties, <u>but we're always there.</u>

    _____

    _____

    b. <u>Do you know the roads around you?</u>

    <u>Do you know the road's around you?</u>

    _____

    _____

4. What if the apostrophe were left off the contraction in the sentence below? How could the sentence be misunderstood?

    I would rather we'd not date.

    _____

    _____

Apostrophe With Singular Possessive

One boy has a pile that blows away.

If you write: The boys pile leaves.

Readers think: More than one boy piles leaves.

You mean: The boy's pile leaves.

> **THE LOGIC**
> Without the apostrophe, a possessive noun seems plural. There seems to be more than one boy. The possessed noun (pile) seems to be a verb; in *The boys pile leaves, pile* is an action of the boys.
>
> **THE RULE**
> To make a singular noun possessive, add *'s*. Example: the *dog's* bone.

PRACTICE

1. Add apostrophes only where necessary to show a possessive word.

    a. Take Bobs books. He hates them.

    b. That books cover is dirty. Those books are clean.

    c. Those girls have bags. That girls bag looks heavy.

2. Circle the correct word to complete each sentence according to its hint.

    a. He borrowed one (friends, friend's) snowboard. (Hint: *Snowboard* is a thing, or noun.)

    b. His (friends, friend's) snowboard down the hill. (Hint: *Snowboard* is an action, or verb.)

The Language Mechanic   Punctuation

YOUR TURN

1. Add apostrophes where necessary to show a possessive word.

    a. That mans best friend is his red setter.

    b. This womans best friend is her golden retriever.

    c. A childs best friend may be his or her teddy bear.

2. In each set, underline the sentence that is correctly written.

    a. The bear's paw has a thorn.

        The bears paw's has a thorn.

        The bears paw has a thorn.

    b. They go with Netties aunts.

        They go with Nettie's aunts.

        They go with Netties aunt's.

3. The following nouns are singular. Make them possessive.

    leader   baby   woman   child   man

4. Write a singular possessive noun that makes sense in the blank. (Use a possessive that requires an *'s*, not *my, your*, etc.)

    a. The __car's__ steering wheel won't turn.

    b. I love _____ hairdo.

    c. We saw _____ uncle.

    d. My _____ teacher is ill.

    e. Our _____ office is hard to find.

The Language Mechanic   Punctuation

CHALLENGE

1. Underline the sentences that are written correctly. Explain what they mean.

   a. We saw the bird's nest in the tree.

   b. We saw the birds nest in the tree.

   c. We saw the birds nest's in the tree.

2. In each blank, write the number of the clue that matches the sentence.

   Clue 1: *Stack* is a noun   **Clue 2**: *Stack* is a verb

   a. The boy's stack flies. _____

   b. The boys stack flies. _____

   Clue 1: *Duck* means avoid.   **Clue 2**: *Floats* means rests on water.

   c. My friend's duck floats. _____

   d. My friends duck floats. _____

   Clue 1: Leaders teach male sheep.

   Clue 2: The conductor has a train that smashes something.

   e. The conductor's train rams. _____

   f. The conductors train rams. _____

Apostrophe With Plural Possessive

You have many uncles, and you plan to visit five of them.

If you write: I will visit five of my uncle's houses.

Readers think: Your uncle has five houses.

You mean: I will visit five of my *uncles'* houses.

> **THE LOGIC**
>
> An apostrophe <u>before</u> the *s* shows that a possessive noun is <u>singular</u>. The possessed noun (*houses*) seems to belong to one uncle!
>
> **RULE 1**
>
> If a plural noun ends in *s*, add only an apostrophe to make it possessive. Example: *five cats' tails*
>
> **RULE 2**
>
> If a plural noun does not end in *s*, add *'s* to make it possessive. Examples: *children's game, deer's horns, people's wishes, men's clothing, sheep's wool.*

PRACTICE

1. Use Rule 1 to make each of the underlined plural nouns possessive.

<u>foxes</u> dens   <u>babies</u> toys   <u>adults</u> jobs   <u>fathers</u> clubs

2. Use Rule 2 to make each of the underlined plural nouns possessive.

<u>men</u> clothing   <u>children</u> games   <u>people</u> heads   <u>deer</u> trails

3. Underline the sentences that are written correctly. Use both rules.

   a. We followed those men's tracks.   c. We followed that mans' tracks.

   b. We followed those mens' tracks.   d. We followed that man's tracks.

The Language Mechanic   Punctuation

YOUR TURN

1. Add an apostrophe or 's where necessary to show a possessive word.

   Rule 1: (plural ending in s)
   a. Those books covers are dirty. Those other books are clean.
   b. Those girls cases look heavy. I met the two sisters father.

   Rule 2: (plural not ending in s)
   c. Put the children coats on the children.
   d. We women saw the other women team yesterday.

2. Label each possessive noun as **S** for singular and **P** for plural.
   a. The teachers' tests are easy. ___
   b. My friend's parents are strict. ___
   c. This house's walls are thin. ___
   d. Both my parents' cars are broken. ___

3. Underline each correctly written sentence.
   a. We saw the five deer's tracks.
   b. We saw those five deers tracks.
   c. We saw those five deers' tracks.

4. Add apostrophes where necessary.
   a. The womens race begins soon.
   b. That womans time is the best.
   c. Childrens story hour is her favorite time.
   d. She holds a childs toy.

5. Make each underlined word into a plural possessive and write it in the blank.
   a. Her <u>friend's</u> clothes fit her. _____
   b. The <u>dog's</u> legs are hurting. _____

6. Fill each blank so all sentences make sense. Use each of the following words once. *(doors, door's, doors')*

   The two front _____ knobs are broken. The back _____ knob needs polishing. The other _____ have no knobs.

CHALLENGE

1. Is the word nest a verb or a noun? Write **V** or **N** in each blank.

    a. I see the bird's nest in the tree. _____

    b. I see the birds nest in the tree. _____

2. For each sentence below, describe (or draw) what the statement means.

    a. The girls seal leaks.

    b. The girl's seal leaks.

    c. The girls' seal leaks.

3. For each clue, write the letter of the statement it describes. (Shift can be a verb meaning <u>to switch</u> or a noun meaning <u>work period</u>.)

    Clue 1: Workers at the ends of the table switch places. _____

    Clue 2: The shift is over for one of the workers. _____

    a. The workers shift ends.

    b. The workers' shift ends.

    c. The worker's shift ends.

The Language Mechanic — Punctuation

Question Mark

A man is coming. You want to know if he is arriving by boat or by plane.

If you write: How is the man coming from overseas.

Readers think: The man's name is How!

You mean this: How is the man coming from overseas?

Howard
(How for short)

THE LOGIC

The reader may not know you are asking a question unless the question mark is there. *How* could be a name.

THE RULE

To show that a sentence asks a question, place a question mark at the end. Also, the following may be used as clues to show a question:
- Question words: *when, where, who, how, what,* and *why.*
- Word order: *Is it* a clam? *It is* a clam.
- Words near the speaker of a quotation: *"You'll let me help?"* she <u>asked</u>.

PRACTICE

1. Match each clue to its sentence.

   Clue 1: "How" is the boy's name.

   Clue 2: You want to know about someone's action.

   a. How is the boy playing? _____   b. How is the boy playing. _____

2. Fill in the ending punctuation. Use "question words" to decide whether to use a question mark.

   a. Hoo is the owl we hear _____
   b. Who is the owl we hear _____

3. Fill in the ending punctuation. Pay attention to the order of the words.

   a. Will they go today _____   c. You can sing _____
   b. They will go today _____   d. Can you sing _____

The Language Mechanic   Punctuation

YOUR TURN

1. Add ending punctuation that makes sense.

   a. Will there be chocolate ___   There will be chocolate ___

   b. Where are we going ___   We are going where they are going ___

   c. You know my sister ___   Do you know my brother ___

   d. He could keep the pet ___   Could he keep the shirt ___

2. In each blank, write the number of the matching clue.

   Clue 1: You wonder what time she will come.   **Clue 2:** You use Wendy's nickname.

   a. Wen is the new girl coming today. _____

   b. When is the new girl coming today? _____

   Clue 1: You give William a command.   **Clue 2:** You ask someone to do something.

   c. Will, you come here. _____   d. Will you come here? _____

3. Add ending punctuation to each sentence. (Note: Sometimes a statement can switch the normal noun-verb order: Happy is she.)

   a. Is he weary _____   d. Is she the one who sleeps _____

   b. Who works _____   e. Who sleeps here _____

   c. Weary is he who works hard _____   f. It is she who sleeps _____

CHALLENGE

1. Decide which sentences are really meant as questions and add a question mark. (Use ! in all the other blanks.)

   a. You said you'd show me how to make gold. How could I do that ___

   b. You spoiled my brand new sneakers. How could you do that ___

   c. He couldn't keep his kitten. Would I take it ___ Would I ___ I was excited to get it.

2. Sometimes people ask a question using the same word order as the statement. (We are there. We are?) Fill each blank with punctuation that makes sense.

   a. "There are fresh rolls," I said. "There are___" she asked. I replied, "There are___

   b. "I want you to have this," I said. "You're giving me your diary ____" she asked.

The Language Mechanic   Punctuation

Exclamation Mark

A bully has been threatening you. You are terrified and want help.

If you write: I'm so scared.

Readers think: You are pretending to be scared.

You mean: I'm so scared!

> **THE LOGIC**
>
> Punctuation works together with text. The sentence above gives a mixed message. Without the exclamation mark, the reader can think you are just pretending. For example, if someone says *"There's a lion in the yard!"* You may not believe it. You say, *"Yeah, I'm really shaking."*
>
> **THE RULE**
>
> Use an exclamation to show real enthusiasm, excitement, or fear. Place an exclamation mark at the end of the exclamation.
>
> **Note:** Sometimes a sentence that looks like a question is really an exclamation: *"Did you ever see such a sight!"*

PRACTICE

1. For each blank, fill in the ending punctuation.

   Clue: Bob and Mark always say how they feel.

   Dad says, "How do you like your new Super Flash robot?"

   a. Bob says, "I love it ___"   b. Mark says, "I guess it's okay ___"

2. Fill in the blanks to best show the writer's feelings.

   a. I sounded totally bored when I said, "Oh, wow ___ I'm so impressed ___"

   b. I thought she was the greatest. I said, "Oh, wow ___ I'm so impressed ___"

The Language Mechanic   Punctuation

YOUR TURN

1. For each blank, fill in the best punctuation.

    a. I hate peas ___ I think I'll throw up.

    b. I can't wait to see her. Hey, there's her ship ___

    c. Here comes the ride ___ I'm too tired to care.

2. Match each feeling to a different statement below.

    A. excited   **B.** bored   **C.** not believing   **D.** scared

    a. There's an alligator in there! _____   d. I'm so excited. Yeah, right. _____

    b. Sure, there's an alligator in there. _____

    c. Hey, I see the ship coming in! _____

3. For each statement, fill in the best punctuation. Use the hints.

    a. Get me some bandages ___ (Hint: You're bleeding.)

    b. Get out of the chair ___ (Hint: You're bored.)

    c. Get out of the way ___ (Hint: You're in a hurry.)

    d. We just won the lottery___ (Hint: That is awesome.)

    e. Sure, we could win the lottery tomorrow ___ (Hint: You think they're dreaming.)

    f. How dare you say that ___ (Hint: You are angry.)

CHALLENGE

1. Joey and Jill need some exclamation marks. Add two exclamation marks for Joey. Add two for Jill. Put the four marks in the best places to show meaning.

    Joey: I've never been on a roller coaster like that. The Banker was awesome. It turned us upside down. It went through five spirals. It was great.

    Jill: I've ridden on lots of coasters. The Banker was awesome for Joey. For me, it was boring. It's the Bounder I can't wait to ride. It takes you high then drops you with a SWOOSH.

2. Some sentences look like questions when the writer is just making a point and doesn't want an answer. Fill blanks with exclamation or question marks.

    a. Where should we sit ___   b. Did you ever see such a bad movie ___

The Language Mechanic — Punctuation

Quotation Marks

The more you listen to the song "Mold," the more you like it.

You write: Mold really grows on you.

Readers think: Fungus is growing on someone!

You mean: "Mold" really grows on you.

THE LOGIC
If titles are not set off with quotation marks, they may appear to mean something else. Instead of a song, *Mold* is taken as regular noun meaning fungus!

THE RULE
Use quotation marks around the titles of poems, songs, short stories, or works of art. (The titles should also be capitalized.)

PRACTICE

1. The following sentences are written correctly. Underline the one title in each sentence.

   a. He read "The Hero" until he fell asleep.

   b. I was looking for "Blue Ice" on a CD until Jake cried, "Here it is!"

2. Add any needed quotation marks to the following sentences. Use logic.

   a. The Tree really grows on you. I like to read it under the tree.

   b. Bonnie is a cool girl. Bonnie is a cool song.

3. In each blank, write the number of the clue that matches the statement.

   Clue 1: She spoke of a story.   **Clue 2:** She spoke of a person.

   a. She said she loved "The Little Child." _____

   b. She said she loved the little child. _____

The Language Mechanic   Punctuation

YOUR TURN

1. The following sentences are written correctly. Underline the titles.

    a. They went to the concert to hear "Bright Patch."

    b. We wanted to find "Brice's Canyon" at the library. "Let's go," I said.

2. Put quotation marks around the titles.

    a. They enjoyed New York because it was a great work of art.
        They saw it in the city of New York.

    b. He loved both parents, but Mama was his favorite.
        She liked many statues, but Papa was her favorite.

    c. David was made of white marble.
        Danny was made of flesh and bone.

3. In each blank, write the number of the clue that describes the statement.

    Clue 1: She was allergic to certain flowers.

    Clue 2: She hated hearing the song.

    a. She said "Smelling Daisies" made her sick. _____

    b. She said smelling daisies made her sick. _____

CHALLENGE

1. Underline each title mentioned below.

    Jon and Sal waited outside by the "Dazed Dolphin" statue. He asked, "Who's going with you to see the play?" She said, "Gerald and Claude." Then she told him they were going to see "Harold and Maude."

2. Put quotation marks around each title. (Hint: The title of a poem is singular; it takes a singular verb.)

    a. Butterflies are enjoyable to see. Butterflies is enjoyable to hear.

    b. Grandparents is fun to watch. Grandparents are fun to watch.

The Language Mechanic   Punctuation

UNIT REVIEW: Punctuation

DIRECTIONS: Add or correct the punctuation where underlined if necessary.

Paintings are Bobby's favorite kind of art. Sculptures are Bonita's favorite. What are the children's plans after school? They are going to the museum.

In the museum, she says, "Let's check out the metals."

He says, "I'd rather look at the paintings. Will you meet me back here in fifteen minutes?"

She says, "Yes, I'll be here."

Bonita finds the metal arts. She sees a sculpture showing five kittens' mittens. She sees one called "Men's Clothing." Then she takes a close look at a sculpture called "Hay Wire." She backs up. "Yikes!" she shouts. She feels something sharp. A part of "Hay Wire" is poking her. The barb's points sting Bonita's back. She's able to pick out most of the points. She goes to meet Bobby.

"I'm over here!" he exclaims. He tells her about the paintings. He describes "Jacob's Ring" and tells how close he got to "The Warrior."

"Good," she says. "I liked the sculptures, too. Let's go." Bobby follows her and notices something. She still has some wire attached.

"Wow!" yells Bobby. "You really did like the sculpture, didn't you? You've decided to take it home!"

They return the wire to the head of the museum. Then they go home tired. The two art lovers' day is over.

9. PUNCTUATION: Comma

Comma in a Series

When you went to the park, you saw lots of grass. You also saw animals and balloons.

If you write: I saw grass animals and balloons.

Readers think: The animals were made of grass!

You mean: I saw grass, animals, and balloons.

> **THE LOGIC**
> Leaving out commas that separate items in a series can confuse your reader. When words are not separated, two things seem to be one. Instead of grass *and* animals, we think of *grass animals*. *Grass* seems to be an adjective modifying *animals*.
>
> **THE RULE**
> A series is a list of things, one after another. Use a comma to separate the things in the series: *"I'll get the hammer, saw, and chisel."* (Use *and* before the last item.)
> • The things can be objects, actions, descriptions, etc.
> • Each thing can be more than one word: *a red ball, a blue box, and a white cube; get ready, get set, and go*

PRACTICE

1. In each blank, write the number of the clue that matches the statement.

   Clue 1: There are three things.   **Clue 2:** There are two things.

   a. We found paper dolls and paints. _____

   b. We found paper, dolls, and paints. _____

2. Add commas to show that there are three things in the series.

   a. The blue tree the yellow bush and the purple cow stand in the field.

   b. We'll build with mud bricks and wood.

The Language Mechanic   Punctuation: Comma

YOUR TURN

1. Add commas to the sentence so that four things are done.

They ditched their homework dyed their hair stayed out late and got grounded.

2. In each blank, write the number of the clue that matches the statement.

Clue 1: He cut three materials.   **Clue 2:** He took three actions.

   a.   He cut the wood, the metal, and the glass. _____

   b.   He cut the wood, worked the metal, and blew the glass. _____

3. In this sentence, there is only one pie: We ate the lemon meringue strawberry cream pie.

Add *and* and/or commas to show the right number of pies.

   a.   We ate the lemon meringue strawberry cream pies. (Hint: there are two pies.)

   b.   We ate the lemon meringue strawberry cream pies. (Hint: there are three pies.)

   c.   We ate the lemon meringue strawberry cream pies. (Hint: there are four pies.)

4. The following paragraph contains series that need commas. Correct it by adding commas where they belong. Pay attention to the story information. It will help you decide how many things are in the series.

I have only one sister and one brother. One day we were all playing with our two cousins. We ran through four places as fast as we could. They were the hall closet bedroom kitchen and bathroom. Dad was mad at Betty Joe and me. He was not mad at my cousins, Mary Sue and Dave.

The Language Mechanic   Punctuation: Comma

CHALLENGE

1. Fill in each blank according to the meaning of the sentence as it is written.

    a. A.J. can make his socks bake a pie and do the dishes.

    The pie is baked by _____.

    b. A.J. can make his socks, bake a pie, and do the dishes.

    The pie is baked by _____.

2. The sentences below seem to be the same. Show two different meanings by putting the commas in different places. (Hint: Each sentence can show three actions or three items.)

    a. You'll get watermelon peel apples and tie straps.

    b. You'll get watermelon peel apples and tie straps.

3. Use the clues below to correct the paragraph sentences. Each numbered clue goes with the sentence of the same number. (Correct the last sentence without a clue.)

    1. Josh had only a frog and a dog that finds birds.
    3. Josh took three different actions (putting three things).
    4. Five things were chased by the frog.
    5. The dog did three things.

    [1]Josh had a bird dog and a frog. [2]Josh got a little mixed up one day. [3]He put the frog on the dog leash himself in the pond and the dog on his bike. [4]The frog chased a car stick squirrel and two birds. [5]The dog wobbled down the street ran into a tree and fell off. [6]Josh made a "ribbit" sound hopped off a rock fell through a lily pad and ended up soaked.

The Language Mechanic   Punctuation: Comma

Commas to Set Off the Year

Day after day, his lunchbox held only vegetables. Then things changed!

You write: On April 23, 2000 candy
                  bars appeared.

Readers think: There were 2000 candy bars
                  in his lunchbox!

You mean: On April 23, 2000, candy bars appeared.

THE LOGIC

Using a comma before and after the year keeps the date separated from other thoughts.

THE RULE

Use a comma before and after the year in a sentence when using the format *month, day, year*.
Example: *The Martians planned a June 14, 2088, invasion of Earth.*
Note: The year is sometimes shown with only two digits and an apostrophe: *'42* instead of 1942 or 2042.

PRACTICE

1. Place commas where needed.

    a. On January 1, 2003 we'll have a party.

    b. We will start planning it on December 1 2002.

2. In each blank, write the number of the matching clue.

    Clue 1: There were nearly 2000 people sick on May 1.

    Clue 2. People were sick on May 1 of the year 1980.

    a. On May 1, 1980 people were sick with the flu. _____

    b. On May 1, 1980, people were sick with the flu. _____

The Language Mechanic   Punctuation: Comma

YOUR TURN

1. Fix each sentence. Remember to place a comma after both the day and the year.

   a. On December 25, 1842 Festus got his first pair of boots.

   b. There were a hundred fools in the April 1, 1960 parade.

   c. The jumping snail was discovered July 2, 2020 in the Goby Sea.

2. It's easy to confuse numbers when they are not separated! Place commas where needed.

   a. Jonathan was born on April 30 1945.

   b. Beula's birthday was June 23 1923.

   c. Peppy was born on September 19 2000.

3. In each blank, write the number of the clue that matches the statement.

   Clue 1: There were 2000 Hondas.   **Clue 2:** The year was 2000.

   a. On August 1, 2000, Hondas covered the streets. _____

   b. On August 1, 2000 Hondas covered the streets. _____

   Clue 1: You can't tell how many Chevies there were.
   Clue 2: There was an odd number of Chevies.

   c. On August 2, 1957 Chevies arrived. _____

   d. On August 2, 1957, Chevies arrived. _____

4. Fill in the blanks to answer the questions.

   We had 25 pets on July 1, '83, when we moved.

   a. Did we have 83 pets when we moved? _____

   b. How is the number '83 being used?

   _____

   _____

The Language Mechanic   Punctuation: Comma

CHALLENGE

1. Add commas where needed. Watch out! Pay attention to the logic of each sentence.

   On November 15 2000 Jake played his last game. Jake set a record for home runs for the year 2000. His friends call him "2000 Homer." It is now June 10 2002. On June 15, 2000 Homer graduates.

2. A comma is sometimes used to show where words are left out. In the following example, the last comma replaces the word *and*.

   We sold thousands of goods at our bakery in one day. We had 5034 donuts on Jan. 20, 1943 when we closed shop.

   (There were 1,943 *donuts* when we closed.)

   In each blank, write the number of the clue that matches the sentence.

   Clue 1: The population more than tripled.

   Clue 2: We can tell in what year gold was found.

   a. The town had only 500 people on December 8, 1700, when gold was struck.

   b. The town had only 500 people in December 8, 1700 when gold was struck.

   What words are replaced by the comma in **b** above? _____

3. Edit the following story by adding needed commas or crossing out unnecessary commas. Pay attention to context clues!

   It was the third day of March in 1963. We had just come from the Lutherville Opera House, built on May 1 1880. That's where we saw the play, "Lutherville in 1902." We wondered if the play had the correct dates for 1902. It said that on September 30, 900, people had been killed in a big town fire. Grandma said she thought it was more like 1000 people. She said it was September 29, 1902 when the fire began.

   The play showed other events of 1902. In July, 1800, new homes were started. Many of those 1800 homes were finished by January 1 1903 so people could move in.

Comma in Address

Your friend is coming to visit at your new house: 449 West Dover Lane, Landing, California. You email the address with commas in the wrong place.

You write: I'm at 449 West Dover, Lane Landing, California.

Readers think: The town is Lane Landing and the street is West Dover.

You mean: I'm at 449 West Dover *Lane*, Landing, California.

> **THE LOGIC**
>
> If you run the parts of an address together, the address may be unreadable. People may never find you!
>
> **THE RULE**
>
> In an address within text, use a comma after the street and one after the city: *The principal lives at 125 Main Street, Hobbesville, Ohio.*
> **Note:** An address used for delivery is written on separate lines. On an envelope or letterhead, the town and state are on a line with the zip code: *449 West Dover Lane*
> *Landing, CA 95000*

PRACTICE

1. Add commas where needed.

   She came to our place at 125 Davis Street Porterstown California. (Hint: The name of the city is Porterstown.)

2. Circle the letter of the address that shows you live on Savage Way in a town in the state of Virginia.

   a. I'm at 206 Savage, Way Circle Flats West, Virginia.
   b. I'm at 206 Savage Way, Circle Flats West, Virginia.
   c. I'm at 206 Savage Way, Circle Flats, West Virginia.
   d. I'm at 206 Savage Way Circle, Flats West, Virginia

The Language Mechanic   Punctuation: Comma

YOUR TURN

1. Add commas to complete the sentence below.

    There is a beautiful house at 1890 Wariner Way Lovell's Place Wyoming.

2. You live in the state of Maryland. Your apartment is on a busy street called Iz Way. Your number, 2000, is at the end of the street. Your city is Outatown. Fill in your address below for a friend who wants to visit you.

    I live at _____.

3. Fill each blank with the letter of the sentence that is described. Do not use the same letter twice. (Hint: Do Clue 1 before Clue 2.)

    Clue 1: His state is not North Carolina. _____

    Clue 2: His street is an alley. _____

    a. He's at 9 Lives Way, Alley Catscan Run, North Carolina.
    b. He's at 9 Livesway Alley, Catscan Run North, South Carolina.
    c. He's at 9 Lives Way Alley, Catscan Run, North Carolina.

4. Add all the commas needed to make the addresses clear. Use the hint and your knowledge of state names. (Hint: *Boulevard*, *Lane*, and *Drive* are parts of street names.)

    We are moving from 1899 Cordova Boulevard Fig Springs California to 13 1/2 Sycamore Drive Pinkertown Arizona. We were thinking of moving to my aunt's house at 1445 Country Lane Baldwin Maine. That was too far, though.

The Language Mechanic

Punctuation: Comma

CHALLENGE

1. Add commas to the address. (Hint: The town below has a sister city called *Kentucky Springs East*.)

Our travel agent was located at 222 East Marble Heights Kentucky Springs West Virginia.

2. Read the story then fill in the blank with the correct address.

I was supposed to send Maggie a check, but I forgot to write the correct address. At 10 years old, I should know better! I'll figure it out. She eats a lot of pizza, but she lives on Cabbage. I live in a state of panic, but she lives in Maine. Oh! I remember that her house number is twice my age. I'll have to look up the zip code for Smithville.

She lives at _____

3. Edit the story by adding commas where needed. Use the clues given below.

Clue 1: One street includes the word *Place*, one includes *Way*.
Clue 2: One person lives in Dobbs Ferry, one lives in East Carthage.

I sent letters to all my pals. Sherry lives at 1345 Jerry Way Atlanta Georgia. Joey is at 45 Cedar Street Dobbs Ferry Texas, and his brother Fred is at 888 Ginger Place Abbsbury Utah. I hope I added enough postage to get each one to its destination from my house at 690 West Drive East Carthage New Jersey.

The Language Mechanic   Punctuation: Comma

Comma After State

You want to describe a small town in the state of New York.

You write: Russell, New York is a quiet town.

Readers think   You are telling Russell
                  that New York City is quiet!

You mean: Russell, New York, is a quiet town.

> **THE LOGIC**
>
> Without the proper commas, both the city and the state could be mistaken for something else.
>
> **THE RULE**
>
> Use a comma before and after the state when using the form *town, state,* to show that the town belongs to that state. Example: *We were in Galveston, Texas, last winter.* If the state is by itself, a comma is not usually needed. Example: *We visited Texas last winter.*

PRACTICE

1. Which of the following are written correctly? Circle their letters.

    a. The city of Jackson, Mississippi is south of us.

    b. The capital of Mississippi is south of us.

    c. The city of Jackson, Mississippi, is south of us.

    d. The city of Jackson Mississippi, is south of us.

2. Add commas where needed.

    a. Let's go to Alaska in the summer.

    b. We'll go to New York New York after that.

    c. I want to see Galveston Texas in the fall.

    d. Lake Placid New York is a fun winter spot.

    e. We'll visit Delaware during springtime.

The Language Mechanic   Punctuation: Comma

YOUR TURN

1. Circle the letter of the sentence that is written correctly.

    a. In Tucson, Arizona Mr. Pan met his flight to Neverland.

    b. In Tucson, Arizona, Mr. Pan met his flight to Neverland.

    c. In Tucson Arizona, Mr. Pan met his flight to Neverland.

2. In each blank, write the number of the clue that matches the statement.

    Clue 1: You tell Adrian about Ohio.   **Clue 2:** Adrian is a town.

    a. Adrian, Ohio is an exciting place to visit! _____

    b. Adrian, Ohio, is an exciting place to visit! _____

3. Edit each sentence so it makes sense. Add commas where needed and cross out unnecessary commas.

    a. Did you know Alaska, is a cold state?   c. He was caught in Parker, City Arizona.

    b. Juneau, Alaska is a northern city.   d. Michael, California, is a great state.

CHALLENGE

1. Add commas only where needed to make sense. Do not use a comma after the state when it begins a new thought: *To the people of Tulsa, Oklahoma is home.*

    a. For the people of Dallas Texas is a great state.

    b. For the people of Dallas Texas ours is a great country.

    c. Monterey California is a special place.

    d. Because it has the city of Monterey California is a special state.

2. A comma may stand for left out words. (In *I had toast for breakfast, pizza for lunch,* the comma means *and I had.*) Discuss the meaning of each sentence.

    a. Bob got his frog in Huntsville, Georgia in a swamp. Bob got his frog in Huntsville, Georgia, in a swamp.

    b. They are visiting Bob in Peakesville, Virginia, later. They are visiting Bob today in Peakesville, Virginia later in Appleton.

The Language Mechanic — Punctuation: Comma

Comma With Noun of Address

Your boss is usually lazy, but not today. You want to tell Bob about it.

You write: The boss is really working Bob.

Readers think: The boss is making Bob work hard!

You mean: The boss is really working, Bob.

> **THE LOGIC**
>
> The comma shows whom you are speaking to. Leaving it out can be confusing.
>
> **THE RULE**
>
> Use a comma to show whom is being spoken to. The comma shows that the person named is being *addressed* (spoken to). That's why the person's name is called a *noun of address*.

PRACTICE

1. The sentences below are written correctly. Circle the letters of the sentences that have a noun of address. Explain how you can tell.

    a. Will, you come to dinner.

    b. Will you come to dinner?

    c. You come to dinner, Will.

    _____

2. In each blank, write the number of the matching clue.

    Clue 1: You want to get to know her.   **Clue 2:** You are telling her something.

    a. I'd like to know, Mrs. Wong. _____

    b. I'd like to know Mrs. Wong. _____

3. You tell Ralph that the light is on. Circle the letter of the correct statement.

    a. The light is on Ralph.   b. The light is on, Ralph.

The Language Mechanic   Punctuation: Comma

YOUR TURN

1. In each blank, write the number of the matching clue.

   Clue 1: You tell the robot to bring something.   **Clue 2:** You want the robot.

   a. Bring that Robot IV. _____   **b.** Bring that, Robot IV. _____

   Clue 1: He'll want lawyers.

   Clue 2: He says which people caused the accident.

   c. He said, "Sue those people who caused the accident." _____

   d. He said, "Sue, those people caused the accident." _____

2. Explain the differences between these two statements:

   a. They failed Ben.   **b.** They failed, Ben.

   _____

   _____

3. Read the sentence below. It could be followed by either **a** or **b**. Explain what is meant by each. (Hint: You are speaking to either a sister or your father.)

   Skydiving is fun, but Mom wouldn't let us do it.

   a. You should try Dad. _____

   b. You should try, Dad. _____

CHALLENGE

1. Correct the following paragraphs by adding or crossing out commas.

   a. I went to a girl named Dorothy and said, "Dorothy has your bicycle been broken for long? John has your bicycle in his garage. I saw Gladys fixing it."

   b. She said, "No, Theodore, that was not my bike. Jeremiah, has one just like it. Maybe it was his."

   c. "It couldn't have been, Jeremiah's bike," said Tootsie. "I saw his bike rolling down the street. He was on it Dorothy!"

The Language Mechanic   Punctuation: Comma

Comma to Separate Quotation From Speaker

The new boy asked Bill what we did first thing in the morning.

If you write: Bill said "The Pledge of Allegiance."

Readers think: Bill said the words of the pledge to Jon!

You mean: Bill said, "The Pledge of Allegiance."

> **THE LOGIC**
> If you don't separate the quoted words from the speaker, they may be read as something else. (Quotation marks can be used to show titles of poems, songs, stories, etc.)
>
> **THE RULE**
> **Part A:** Separate the quoted words from the words showing who is speaking those words (or singing, shouting, etc.). The comma shows that the words in quotation marks were the actual words said by the speaker named before or after the comma.
>   *She said,* "Hi."   "Hello*," he replied.*   BUT   *He said we could go.*
> **Part B:** Do not add a comma after the quote if it is a question or exclamation.
>   *"What a wonderful gift!" she exclaimed. "How did you know?" she asked.*
> **Part C:** Be careful. Some words have quotation marks to show that they are titles. Do not use a comma with these.
>   *Joseph sang "Hayride" with us.* (But: *Joseph called, "Hey, ride with us!"*)

PRACTICE (A, B, C)

1. Add commas where needed. (Use Rule Part A)

   a. "Go home" they said.   b. "In that case" he said "I will go."

2. Add the correct punctuation where needed. (Use Rule Parts A and B)

   a. "I'm so excited __" she yelled.   b. She exclaimed __ "Get out!"

3. Cross out the choice that is NOT written correctly. (Use Rule Part C)

   a. She said the, "Pledge of Allegiance."   c. "He sang the words to "Jingle Bells."

   b. She said, "I pledge allegiance."   d. He felt good. "It's a great day," he sang.

The Language Mechanic   Punctuation: Comma

YOUR TURN: PART A

1. Circle the sentence that is written correctly.

   a. She said "My hair is blue."   c. She said, "My hair is blue."

   b. She, said "My hair is blue."   d. She said "My, hair is blue."

2. Cross out the sentence that is NOT written correctly.

   a. He says, we will get paid.   b. He says, "We will get paid."

3. Correct the following paragraphs by adding commas as needed.

   "I wonder where those shoes are," she said.

   "I suppose you mean the magic ones" he replied. "They are in the closet. Does Father need to be rescued again?"

   "No" she answered. "He's doing fine by himself. He's fighting the purple ewe this time" she said. "I just thought I'd have the shoes resoled."

YOUR TURN: PART B

1. Circle the sentences that are written correctly.

   a. "Where is the car," she asked.   c. She asked, "What has happened?"

   b. "I don't know!" he shouted.   d. "Someone stole it," he exclaimed.

2. Add punctuation where needed.

   a. She asked where the class was.

   b. She asked "Where is our class?"

   c. "It's way over in Towville" he exclaimed.

   d. "When does it begin" she asked.

   e. He shouted "It's already started!"

The Language Mechanic Punctuation: Comma

3. Correct the story by crossing out or adding punctuation.

The boy's fingers were rolled up into tight balls. "You called me a wimp!," Lane shouted at the girl.

Jana said calmly "I did no such thing."

"But they all heard you say it!" he insisted.

"Are you sure?", she asked. "They didn't listen very carefully. I said that Blane was a sissy, not you!"

Lane relaxed. "You did," he asked. "Then I'm sorry." He wondered who Blane was.

YOUR TURN: PART C

1. In each blank, write the number of the clue that is true for the statement.

Clue 1: It shows a quote. **Clue 2:** It shows a title.

Clue 3: It shows neither.

a. She sang the blues. _____

b. She sang, "The blues get me down." _____

c. She sang "The Blues." _____

2. One statement shows Mark's exact words. Underline those exact words.

a. Mark said the "Gettysburg Address."

b. Mark said his speech for us.

c. Mark said, "The Gettysburg Address was given by Lincoln."

3. Add commas where they belong.

a. He recited "The Stars and Stripes." She said "The stars and stripes are colorful."

b. "You're in my blue heaven" sung Mary. "My Blue Heaven" was sung by Mary.

The Language Mechanic   Punctuation: Comma

CHALLENGE

1. Place commas where needed.

   a. She said "The Rose Story" was her favorite. I said it wasn't mine.

   b. I asked. "Which story did you tell?" He said "It was the long one."

   c. "What was the name of that movie?" I asked. "The Coast" he said.

   d. He chanted "Wipe that silly smile off your face" as she sang "Row Your Boat."

2. In each blank, write the number of the clue that describes the statement.

   Clue 1: He sang the whole song.   **Clue 2:** He sang only part of a song.

   a. He sang "Grandma Got Run over by a Reindeer." _____

   b. He sang, "Grandma got run over by a reindeer." _____

3. Fix the story by adding or crossing out commas.

   I asked Monica to read, "Terror at Sea." It is about a captain whose ship goes through a storm. He gets courage by singing part of "Old Captains Never Die." The first line gives him strength as he sings "Never fearing, keep on steering."

   I asked Monica "Where is the ship headed?"

   "To Greenland," she replied.

   I had seen a play about this same story. It was called, "Going South."

   "In the play," I said "I think the ship was headed south."

   She said "Well, the book says, it goes north." She finished telling, "Terror at Sea."

   I told Monica something I remembered from the play. The captain had said, "We shouldn't have sailed the ship this way." The mate said "It's really going south now."

   "Oh, I get it!," Monica laughed. "When something goes south, it means it's going badly. It's a play on words."

   Well, that was one play she saw that I didn't.

The Language Mechanic   Punctuation: Comma

Comma After Introductory Words

Someone asks if there are mean kids at your school. You want to say "No."

You write: No kids are nice there.

Readers think: There are no kids that are nice at your school!

You mean: No, kids are nice there.

> **THE LOGIC**
>
> A comma makes it clear that the first word is an introduction. If the comma is missing, the first word may change the meaning.
>
> **THE RULE**
>
> An introductory word is at the beginning of the sentence to introduce the thought. *Yes, no,* and *well* are common introductory words. (*However* and *suddenly* are some others.) Use a comma after an introductory word to separate it from the main thought. *"Yes, snuggling up with a tiger can be dangerous." Yes* is the introductory word, and it answers a question.

PRACTICE

1. Put a comma after each word used as an introductory word.

   a. Yes my dog is a hound.   d. Yes they are dried grapes.

   b. No he doesn't eat grapes.   e. No day is bad for dancing.

   c. Well he might eat raisins.   f. Wellness is a good thing.

2. Circle the letter of the statement that goes with the clue.

   Clue: Those who are healthy can get sick.

   a. Well, people can get sick.

   b. Well people can get sick.

The Language Mechanic   Punctuation: Comma

YOUR TURN

1. Add a comma after each introductory word.

   a. Do you have a pencil? Yes I have a pencil.

   b. How about a book? No I don't have a book.

2. Place a comma only after the word used as an introductory word.

   a. Yes and no are words we learn quickly.

   b. Yes we learn them fast and well.

3. How should a mother answer her child's question below? Circle the letter of your choice.

   Question: Can I play in the street?

   a. "No bones are easily broken."   b. "No, bones are easily broken."

4. Below are a question and two different answers. One means *yes* and the other means *no*. Write *yes* or *no* in each blank to show which is which.

   Question: Should I leave the dogs at home?

   a. No dogs are allowed here. _____   b. No, dogs are allowed here. _____

The Language Mechanic   Punctuation: Comma

CHALLENGE

1. In each blank, write the number of the matching clue.

   Clue 1: Children of any size understand kindness.

   Clue 2: *However* is an introductory word.

   a. However, small children understand kindnesses. _____

   b. However small, children understand kindness. _____

2. Correct the paragraph by adding commas after any word used as an introductory word. (Hint: *Well* can also mean to grow or fill.)

   Yes a person can lift a heavy car off a loved one. However it doesn't mean the person has to be built like Arnold Schwarzenegger. Why? Well it's because your body pumps a lot of energy when you suddenly get scared. Let's say something heavy falls on your brother. He is pinned beneath it. Suddenly you have to do something. Yes you have to get that thing off him fast! You feel the strength well up in you. You heave the thing up. Your brother crawls out.

The Language Mechanic   Punctuation: Comma

Comma With Conjunctions

You went grocery shopping. The freezer in the store was broken.

You write: We found everything but the ice cream was melted.

Readers think: Everything except the ice cream was melted!

You mean: We found everything, but the ice cream was melted.

> **THE LOGIC**
>
> The comma shows that the words *but, and,* or *or* are used to make two sentences into one. Above, *but* is taken to mean except.
>
> **THE RULE**
>
> Join two related sentences by using a comma and a word such as *or, and,* or *but*: *She can catch a softball, and she can bake a cake.*
> Each part of the new sentence is an independent clause. An independent clause has both a subject and a verb. The joining word *(and, but, or)* is a conjunction.
> Another way to state the rule is this: Use a comma before the conjunction joining independent clauses.
> **Note:** Don't use a comma if there are NOT two independent causes: *She can catch a softball and throw a party.* (*throw a party* has no separate subject)

PRACTICE

1. Statements **a** and **b** are both written correctly. One statement has a conjunction joining two independent clauses. Circle the letter of that statement. Underline each clause within that statement.

   a. We had lunch, and we ate all the cookies.

   b. We had lunch and ate all the cookies.

2. Underline the statement that joins two sentences. Add a comma where it belongs. (Hint: Each part must have both a subject and a verb.)

   a. He rode into town with the bad guys, took off, and never came back again.

   b. He rode into town and then left.

   c. He rode into town and she left.

The Language Mechanic   Punctuation: Comma

YOUR TURN

1. In each pair of sentences, place a comma where it is needed.

    a. He will either shoot the film or run the lights. He will run them or she will run them.

    b. She must come today or we will be sad. She must come today or be sad.

    c. They tripped the boy and my cousin Jan. They tripped the boy and my cousin fell.

    d. I am ready for fun and he is ready for work. I am good and ready for sunshine.

2. In each blank, write the number of the matching clue.

    Clue 1: The day was both cold and wet.

    Clue 2: It was the people that were wet.

    a. The day was cold, and wet people huddled inside. _____

    b. The day was cold and wet. People huddled inside. _____

    Clue 1: We heard that all of them are new except two.

    Clue 2: We heard all of them, but there are two that are new.

    c. I heard all but two are new. _____

    d. We heard all, but two are new. _____

3. One of the statements below needs a comma. Place it where needed.

    a. You read our lesson but we're confused.

    b. You read our story but were confused.

4. In each blank, write the number of the matching clue.

    Clue 1: He knows that both flying squirrels and flying lemurs glide.

    Clue 2: He personally knows squirrels. Lemurs glide.

    a. He knows flying squirrels and flying lemurs actually glide. _____

    b. He knows flying squirrels, and flying lemurs actually glide. _____

The Language Mechanic   Punctuation: Comma

CHALLENGE

1. For discussion: How would a comma before the word in italics make the meaning different?

   Example: We'll leave those square holes *but* fill those round ones.

   As written, *we* are the ones who fill the round ones. With a comma after *holes,* we are telling you to fill the round ones.

   a. Go see him run the race *and* bike down the canyon.

   b. He was unable to climb up *so* he could see down below.

   c. She thinks Jack is away *but* John is home. (Hint: Jack could be a nickname for John.)

Commas With Appositives—Words That Explain

You want to ask someone if Minnie's best friend, Glen, is in school.

You write: Is Glen her best friend in school?

Readers think: You're asking if Glen is the best friend Minnie has in school.

You mean: Is Glen, her best friend, in school?

> **THE LOGIC**
>
> Without commas to set it off, the explanation becomes part of the main sentence. With commas, the words *her best friend* tell who Glen is.
>
> **THE RULE**
>
> Use commas to separate a word from its description. The explaining words are called an *appositive* (think of them as in *a position* next to the word they explain). Use a comma on either side of the appositive, unless it ends the sentence.

PRACTICE

1. Underline the sentence that is written correctly.

   a. My dog a German shepherd is full of energy.

   b. My dog, a German shepherd is full of energy.

   c. My dog, a German shepherd, is full of energy.

   d. My dog, a German, shepherd is full of energy.

2. In each blank, write the number of the clue that matches the statement.

   Clue 1: You are talking to the captain.

   Clue 2: Captain Crispy is your favorite cereal.

   a. Captain Crispy, my favorite cereal, is running out. _____

   b. Captain Crispy, my favorite cereal is running out. _____

The Language Mechanic   Punctuation: Comma

YOUR TURN

1. In each set, cross out the sentence that is NOT written correctly.

    a.   The fire truck a big red machine screamed past us.

           The fire truck, a big red machine, screamed past us.

           The fire truck was a big red machine screaming past us.

    b.   Our uncle saw a very large man eat the whole thing.

           Our uncle a very large man can eat the whole thing.

           Our uncle, a very large man, can eat the whole thing.

2. Circle the letter of the sentence that is correctly written (each has a different meaning). Fix the other sentence by placing commas where they belong.

    a.   Felix gave his father a black cat as a surprise.

    b.   Felix gave his father a black cat a surprise.

3. In each blank, write the number of the clue that matches the statement.

    Clue 1: You are talking to Ginger about your pet.

    Clue 2: Ginger is your pet.

    a.   Ginger, my pet came to me. _____

    b.   Ginger, my pet, came to me. _____

    Clue 1: You wonder if John is the dentist. **Clue 2:** You know John is the dentist.

    c.   Is John the dentist working on you? _____

    d.   Is John, the dentist, working on you? _____

4. Which statement shows that the writer knows George is hairy? Circle its letter.

    a.   Is George the hairy jungle beast swinging through the trees?

    b.   Is George, the hairy jungle beast, swinging through the trees?

    c.   Is George, the jungle beast, swinging through the trees?

The Language Mechanic   Punctuation: Comma

CHALLENGE

1. Circle the letter of the statement that means this: We gave the monkey to her friend.

    a.   We gave her friend, the monkey, a small pet.

    b.   We gave her friend the monkey, a small pet.

Circle the statement that means this: I put a lot of spicy beans on the food.

    c.   I put on the food a lot of spicy beans.

    d.   I put on the food, a lot of spicy beans.

2. In each blank, write the number of the matching clue.

    Clue 1: Joey was only two feet tall, while Cheri was seven feet tall.

    Clue 2: Cheri was seven feet tall and was two feet taller than Joey.

    a.   Joey was five feet shorter than Cheri. _____

    b.   Joey was five feet, shorter than Cheri. _____

3. Add commas to separate appositives from the surrounding words.

    a.   It was a dark night in Roverton, my home town. Rascal my favorite mutt was whining at the door. Rascal wanted to come in because one of his shows, "Dog King," was on. We three Sis, Rascal, and I watched the show.

    b.   Dog King was fighting off his enemy, Duke. Duke was the meanest animal around. He chased the biggest cars Cadillacs with his two pals, Ring and Spot. Dog King gave his enemy a good snarl. He gave his friend a shepherd a happy bark.

    c.   Rascal was happy to see Dog King getting treats from his human. Rascal looked at his dish an empty bowl. He looked at his owners Sis and me. We gave in. His favorite treat a dog biscuit was placed in his bowl.

The Language Mechanic   Punctuation: Comma

Comma With Introductory Dependent Clause

You think it's fun to slide down a hill when there is snow.

You write: When there is snow sliding
                 down, a hill is fun.

Readers think: Hills are fun when the snow is sliding!

You mean: When there is snow, sliding down a hill is fun.

> **THE LOGIC**
>
> The comma helps show the reader which words belong together. If the words run together, the reader gets the wrong meaning.
>
> **THE RULE**
>
> When a dependent clause comes before the independent clause, place a comma after the dependent clause: *After the show ended, we went home.*
>
> - Clause: A group of words having a subject and a verb. *The show ended* and *after the show ended* are both clauses.
>
> - Independent clause: A clause that could be a sentence by itself: *The show ended.*
>
> - Dependent clause: A clause that cannot stand alone as a sentence: *After the show ended*. The word *After* shows that the clause depends on other words. A dependent clause may begin with a word such as *after, if, while, when, since,* or *unless*.

PRACTICE

1. In each sentence, place a comma after the dependent clause.

   a. After we eat the table is cleared.

   b. While it is light we can read.

   c. If we see them frown we sing louder.

2. Cross out the sentence that is NOT written correctly.

   a. Unless we eat fast we will miss the game.

   b. Unless we eat fast, we will miss the game.

   c. We will miss the game unless we eat fast.

© 2001 The Critical Thinking Co.™ • www.criticalthinking.com • 800-458-4849

The Language Mechanic   Punctuation: Comma

YOUR TURN

1. Add commas where needed.

  a. We were wet after the rain.

  b. After it rained we went out.

  c. Since we were ready we went swimming.

  d. We saw the show after it got dark.

2. Rewrite each sentence so the independent clause comes first. Don't forget the comma! **Example:** I get mad when he yells. <u>When he yells, I get mad.</u>

  a. I've missed him since he left. _____

  _____

  b. I had fun while we were catching toads. _____

  _____

3. In each blank, write the number of the matching clue.

  Clue 1: He flew to Bob silently.   **Clue 2:** He flew without telling Bob.

  a. Without a word, to Bob he flew. _____

  b. Without a word to Bob, he flew. _____

4. For each sentence, tell who is doing the throwing and what is being thrown.

  a. When the pitcher throws, Bob will catch.

  Who throws? _____ What? _____

  b. When the bull throws Bob, catch him.

  Who throws? _____ What? _____

5. Explain how these two sentences are different in meaning.

  a. If you pay next week, you'll be a partner.

  b. If you pay, next week you'll be a partner.

  _____

  _____

The Language Mechanic   Punctuation: Comma

CHALLENGE

1. Show two ways the same words can have different meanings. Add a comma in a different place in each sentence. Then explain what is meant by each sentence.

   a.   After it rains out the worms come.

   b.   After it rains out the worms come.

   _____

   _____

   _____

2. Correct the story by adding commas where needed.

   a.   When you bring your skateboard we can go to the park. Unless it's raining we'll use the outdoor skate ramp. If it is raining we can use the new inside ramp. I can't wait! You can show me how to do the Lobbaloony trick if you know it. I saw it at the park last week. As soon as I learn it I'll have to show my brother, Dan. If I know him he'll be really jealous!

   b.   I'm just beginning to get some air when I fly up the ramp. After I land I'm so proud of myself. Do you remember last month? I couldn't even ride on flat ground! Since you've been teaching me I'm almost as good as Dan.

   c.   After I master the basic moves I want to learn to do flips. Let me know when you think I'm ready. Before I try that maybe I should get some life insurance!

UNIT REVIEW: Comma

DIRECTIONS: Correct the following paragraphs by adding or crossing out commas.

June 1995

I rush up the steep hillside and I look over the top. Didn't I just see a wobbly old woman? I noticed her lace scarf and her cane. The cane would slip on the rocks or it would sink in the mud as she climbed.

I run down the path to the park at 123 East Drive Carson New York. All I see is a young gardener bending over the flowers rocks and shrubs. "Did you see that old lady?" I pant.

"No I didn't see anyone," a voice replies from under a large hat. The gardener turns rises and walks away. I still can't see the face but something is familiar. "Excuse me Sir," I say. "Have we met?"

The gardener doesn't look back but points upward. I see a brick archway with some words on it. It tells me that it was built on February 1 1955 and that I am in the "Garden of Youth." I read aloud "The young become wise, and the old become young."

I look where the gardener had been. I see yellow lace lying by a cane and I suddenly understand.

Am I now wise or just crazy? I am not sure but I know one thing. I am coming back to the park in Carson New York when I get old.

DIRECTIONS: Correct the following paragraphs by adding or crossing out commas.

May 2060

It is now February 1 2060 and I move very slowly. I feel a chill so I wrap my blue sweater around me. I pick up my cane as I head out of my house at 22 King Street Carson New York. It looks like it has rained. I almost fall as my cane dances off the sidewalk a slippery sheet of cement. Something stirs in my memory. I slowly make my way to 123 East Drive. After pulling my sweater tight I struggle up the slope.

I make it to the top and then head for the clearing below. When I get to the garden, I stop. Is someone shouting at me? No it's probably my imagination. At my age, the ears do funny things.

"The plants are lovely" I say to myself. I stoop to smell the flowers a mixture of pinks and purples. A strange feeling comes over me. I can feel my aches pains and other ailments leaving my body!

"Did you see that old woman Miss?" a breathless boy is saying to me. I start to reply when I notice my hands. They are smooth and young! I am speechless. All I can do is point to the archway as I leave my sweater and cane among the flowers.

10. FRIENDLY LETTER: Greeting and Closing

Capitals and Punctuation in Greeting (and Body)

You want to ask Jack if there is any time when he needs help.

You write: Dear Jack is there any time you need help

Readers think: Jack is someone who is always there to help.

You mean: Dear Jack,
Is there any time you need help?

THE LOGIC

Using the wrong format for the greeting and body of a letter can be confusing (especially if punctuation is also left off, as above). The words *Dear Jack is there* could all be a statement about Jack. When written *Dear Jack, Is there* the comma is used like a noun of address. It introduces the next part.

THE RULE

Use correct format for the greeting and body of a note or letter.
- Capitalize the greeting and words used as a name.
- Use a comma after the greeting.
- Start the body of the letter on a new line.
- Capitalize the first word of the body of the letter and use normal sentence capitalizaton and punctuation within the letter body.

PRACTICE

1. Underline the greeting that is written correctly.

   a. dear Sal,   **b.** Dear Sal   **c.** Dear Sal,

2. In each blank, write the number of the matching clue.

   Clue 1: I will eat the cake from my friends.

   Clue 2: My friends will eat my cake because I am on a diet.

   a. My dear friends have a chocolate cake for me. _____

   b. My dear friends,
   Have a chocolate cake for me. _____

Capitals and Punctuation in Closing (and Body)

You are Joe. You write a note to say that Sue doesn't love Stan, Shelly does.

You write: She doesn't love Stan. Shelly does love Joe.

Readers think: Shelly loves Joe!

You mean: She doesn't love Stan. Shelly does.
                 Love, Joe

Shelly Joe

THE LOGIC

Using the wrong format for the body and closing of a letter can cause confusion. (Without correct formatting, *Shelly does love Joe* could all be one sentence!)

THE RULE

Use correct format for the body and closing of a note or letter.
- Use normal sentence punctuation and capitalization in the body.
- Place the closing on a new line and capitalize it.
- Use a comma after the closing. (Some common closings include *Sincerely, Yours truly, Love, Always, Regards,* and *Eagerly*.)
- Place your name on a new line.

Here is an example of proper format for greeting, body, and closing of a friendly letter:

Dear John,

I hope you are finding all the clues in Texas. I am finding the ones in California. When we get them all, let's meet in Arizona.

                                    Love,
                                    Jennifer

PRACTICE

1. In each blank, write the number of the matching clue.

   Clue 1: Mary writes this note.

   Clue 2: Everyone loves Mary.

   a. You know we all do love Mary. _____

   b. You know we all do.
      Love,
      Mary _____

The Language Mechanic   Friendly Letter

YOUR TURN

1. For each pair, circle the choice that should be rewritten in letter format. (Option: Write circled choices in letter format on another sheet of paper.)

   a. My Dear Albert Does everything for me have to be difficult?

   My dear Albert does everything for me because he loves me.

   b. My dearest Sofia has a lovely picture of her brother. She will always love George.

   My dearest Sofia has a lovely picture come for me? Bring it soon love George.

   c. You haven't been here for days. I hope to see you today eagerly Manny.

   You haven't been here for days. I hope today you'll come eagerly with Manny.

2. One choice is written correctly. Circle the letter of the choice that should be written in letter format (a or b). Rewrite the body and closing correctly.

   a. I'd love to be a writer. That's what I plan to be your friend Jasper

   b. In the other play, I was your friend Oscar. In this play, I'll be your friend Jasper.

                                                        August 10, 2005

   Dear Jennifer,

   _____

   _____

                                   _____

                                   _____

3. Add punctuation and capitals to fix the following letter.

                                                        Nov. 12, 2001

   dear tommy

   we loved your play. We all laughed hard! Let us know when you'll do it again

                                        sincerely

                                        jenny

The Language Mechanic   Friendly Letter

CHALLENGE

1. In each blank, write the number of the matching clue.

　Clue 1: The dying plants belong to Mr. Sparkles.

　Clue 2: Mr. Sparkles is being told about the plants.

　a.　Dear Mr. Sparkles, Plants are dying. What should I do? Sincerely, Mahesh ____

　b.　Dear Mr. Sparkles' plants are dying. He will be sad. ____

　Rewrite the letter above in correct format.

　　July 7, 2001

　　_____

　　_____

　　_____

　　_____

2. Underline the choice that is written correctly. Rewrite the other choice in letter format.

　a.　Dear Jake I hope someone is having a good time skiing. I'm not yours truly Mag

　b.　Dear Jake is my new love. I'm not yours truly, Chris.

　　February 10, 1002

　　_____

　　_____

　　_____

3. The following paragraph could have different meanings, depending on how it is formatted, capitalized, and punctuated. On a separate paper, show two different ways it could be formatted. Describe their meanings.

　　My dear cousin Ann is naming her new dog after me! She doesn't think her dad will like him. When he sees him, he will love Cary

UNIT REVIEW: Friendly Letter

DIRECTIONS: Correct the letter below by changing punctuation and capitalization.

September 15, 2005

dear mamie

we wish you could see the beautiful sky here! It looks like someone painted it! The sun almost bleeds into the blue. The puffy clouds are like cotton absorbing the orange and pink. We'll bring you a photograph soon.

love

lonny and tyke

DIRECTIONS: Under the second date, rewrite the letter below in correct format.

October 1, 3050

My dearest eduardo please consider my suggestion. We are from two different planets, but that shouldn't matter. You could get used to living on Tarmon. I'm sure you understand why I can't live on your planet of Swarmagon eaters your Swarmagon snooki

October 1, 3050

11. SPELLING AND VOCABULARY

Confused Word Pairs

You are tired and want to get horizontal for a nap.

If you write: I will lay down on the bed.

Readers think: You are putting goose feathers on the bed.

You mean: I will *lie* down on the bed.

> **THE LOGIC**
>
> Two words may seem much the same but mean very different things. The verb *lay* needs a noun after it. If there is no noun, the reader may take *down* as goose feathers!
>
> **THE RULE**
>
> Use the word that means exactly what you want to say. Every letter matters! To help you do the exercises, use the definitions of word pairs on page 132.

PRACTICE

1. Underline each correct word in parentheses.

    a. She will (lie, lay) on a sofa. She will (lie, lay) her head on a pillow.

    b. He (sits, sets) the table for dinner. He (sits, sets) down to eat.

    c. She (can, may) lift the weights because she's strong. They (can, may) watch TV because they have behaved well.

    d. I know how to sew, so I'll (learn, teach) him how. I don't know how to cook, so I'll (learn, teach) how.

    e. She doesn't have a skirt, so I'll (lend, borrow) her one. I don't have a skirt, so I'll (lend, borrow) one from her.

    f. I like my school, so I won't (leave, let) it. Name calling shouldn't hurt me, so I won't (leave, let) it.

    g. You must (rise, raise) from the bed. You must (rise, raise) yourself from the bed.

DEFINITIONS

lay: to place. *Lay* must have a direct object (something that receives the action).

You can lay yourself down.

You can lay a pencil on the desk.

(Note: The word *lay* can be confusing because it is also the past tense of the verb *to lie!*)

lie: to be in a resting position, as on a bed or to tell an untrue thing; *Lie* does not need a direct object:

You should lie down.

He will lie on the couch.

sit: to be seated or to be located. Sit needs no direct object (something that receives the action):

You should sit down.

We will sit.

set: to place or to put in place or to adjust as a clock. Set must have a direct object:

You should set yourself down.

may: has permission
can: is able

teach: help to learn
learn: get to know how

lend: let someone use
borrow: use someone else's

leave: go or allow to remain
let: allow to

raise: cause to move upward. *Raise* must be followed by a direct object:
  They raise the flag.
rise: move upward. *Rise* needs no direct object:
  The flag will rise.

The Language Mechanic Spelling/Vocabulary

YOUR TURN

1. In each blank, write the number of the matching clue.

    Clue 1: Hal owns the books.   **Clue 2:** Hal does not own the books.

    a. Hal will lend the books so I can read them. _____

    b. Hal will borrow the books so I can read them. _____

2. In each blank, write the correct word: *let/leave, rise/raise, set/sit*

    a. Don't have the girls help us. Please _____ us do it alone. We can't help you, so _____ us. Do it alone.

    b. They will _____ the *Titanic* from the icy waters. The *Titanic* will _____ from the icy waters.

    c. He will _____ in a chair and _____ his alarm clock.

3. Cross out one underlined word in each sentence. Above it, write a word that makes sense.

    a. He <u>lays</u> his head down as he <u>lays</u> in bed.

    b. He <u>may</u> have a cookie if he <u>may</u> reach it.

CHALLENGE

1. In each blank, write the number of the matching clue.

    Clue 1: Teachers get to know names of students.

    Clue 2: Teachers help students learn names.

    a. They teach students names. _____   b. They learn students' names. _____

2. In each blank, write the correct word: *lie, lies, lay,* or *lays.*

    a. People who make feather pillows _____ down in the pillow cover. People who are tired _____ down on the bed.

    b. He _____ in bed. She _____ sheets on the couch. He _____ about his age. She _____ down on the floor to rest.

Homophones and Other Similar Words

You want to get close to your true love.

If you write: Give me a kiss, my deer.

Readers think: You are talking to an animal!

You mean: Give me a kiss, my *dear*.

THE LOGIC
If you spell a word wrong, the reader may get the wrong idea. Having the same sound doesn't mean the words are the same. Spelling makes all the difference!

THE RULE
Homophones are words that sound the same but have different spellings. Spell homophones and other similar words correctly, as shown on page 135. Every letter matters!

(**Note:** Homophones that begin with silent consonants are shown on page 142.)

PRACTICE

1. Circle each correct word shown in parentheses.

   a. I love bears. He found three (four, for) me. I want three or (four, for).

   b. Come (to, two, too) town with your (to, two, too) hats. Bring mine, (to, two, too).

   c. He can (here, hear) my voice (here, hear) in the house.

   d. I can see that (its, it's) a very tall giraffe. I can't see (its, it's) eyes.

   e. They went over (there, their) for vacation. They went over (there, their) plans for vacation.

   f. Will they (see, sea) the ship on the (see, sea)?

   g. The new baby is their first (sun, son). He gets too hot in the (sun, son).

   h. The paths (our, are) not paved, but (our, are) driveway is.

HOMOPHONES
Similar Sounding Words

are/our
are: form of the verb "to be" (we are going)
our: belonging to us

ate/eight
ate: past tense of *eat*
eight: one more than seven

beat/beet
beat: win over
beet: a vegetable

for/four
for: toward
four: one more than three

hear/here
hear: what ears can do
here: in this place

it's/its
it's: it is
its: belonging to it

might/mite
might: showing possibility, or strength
mite: something tiny

not/knot
not: a negative word
knot: place where rope is tied tightly; action of tying

pail/pale
pail: bucket
pale: nearly white

pore/pour
pore: a small opening
pour: to flow liquid

raise/rays
raise: to lift (something)
rays: beams of light

right/rite/write
right: not wrong
rite: ceremony
write: form letters

sea/see
sea: a large body of water
see: detect with the eyes

sight/site
sight: vision
site: place

soar/sore
soar: glide
sore: painful

son/sun
son: male child
sun: Earth's star

their/there
their: belonging to them
there: that place

throne/thrown
throne: royal seat
thrown: past tense of the verb *throw*

to/to/two
to: toward
too: also
two: one more than one

The Language Mechanic　　　　　　　　　　　　　　　　　　　　　　Spelling/Vocabulary

YOUR TURN

1. Circle the sentence that gives the most information.

    a. The show runs for days.　　　　b. The show runs four days.

2. Draw a line from each sentence to a word that makes sense in the blank. Use each word once.

    a. A blind man will come over _____ .　　　see

    b. A blind man will come_____ the band.　　　sea

    c. The deaf man will go to _____ the ship.　　　hear

    d. The deaf man will go to _____ in a ship.　　　here

3. Write the correct word in each blank.

    a. Jon loves cookies. We will bring a couple _____ him. (to, two, too)

    Jon loves cookies. We will bring him _____. (to, two, too)

    Jon loves cookies. We will bring him fudge, _____. (to, two, too)

    b. The toad was hit, but ____ okay. There is just a scratch on ____ leg. (its, it's)

    c. The house is over _____ . The moon is over _____ house. (there, their)

    d. Those _____ from the sun encouraged us to _____ our bodies from bed. (raise, rays)

    e. Your roads _____ long like _____ roads. (our, are)

4. In each blank, write the number of the matching clue.

    Clue 1: Mama was like a queen.　　　**Clue 2:** Mama had to catch her seat.

    a. The chair was throne to Mama. _____

    b. The chair was thrown to Mama. _____

The Language Mechanic   Spelling/Vocabulary

CHALLENGE

1. Below, two sentences are broken up. Draw a line from each beginning to its logical ending. (Hint: They went to get a plate at the buffet lunch.)

    a.   They got their first   because they were fastest.

    b.   They got there first   plate, and they'll get another later.

2. In each blank, write the number of the matching clue.

    Clue 1: Their light beams shine.

    Clue 2: They bring up their child.

    a.   The aliens raise Flash on the ship. _____

    b.   The aliens' rays flash on the ship. _____

3. Describe the meaning of each sentence below.

    a.   Your parents are teachers, and your cousins are actors.

    b.   Your parents, our teachers, and your cousins are actors.

    _____
    _____

4. Either word could finish the sentence below. Explain why.

    Did he tie the rope? He did (knot, not). _____
    _____
    _____

5. Choose one or more pairs of homophones below. Use each pair correctly in a sentence. Use a dictionary, and another paper, if necessary.

    pore/pour; sore/soar; pale/pail; mite/might; site/sight; ate/eight

    _____
    _____
    _____
    _____

Spelling Plural and Singular Nouns

The little kids had to sit and watch the news instead of playing outside.

If you write: We made the childs watch.

Readers think: You created a timepiece for children.

You mean: We made the *children* watch.

THE LOGIC
Using the wrong spelling for a plural noun can suggest a different meaning. (Even if *child's* has no apostrophe, some readers might think you meant to use a possessive noun.)

THE RULE
Use the correct spelling to change the singular form of a noun to its plural form. Use the list below to help you do the exercises.
- For regular nouns, add *s*.
- For nouns ending in *s*, *ss*, *x*, *ch*, or *sh*, add *es*.
- For nouns ending in *y*, change *y* to *i* and add *es*.
- For nouns ending in *f* or *fe*, change the *f* or *fe* to *v* and add *es*: *knife, knives*.
- For special nouns, learn the spellings: *man/men, woman/women, child/children, person, people*
- For some nouns, spell the singular and plural the same: *sheep, deer, fish*.

PRACTICE

1. Circle the correct word in parentheses.

    a. That (girl, girls) doesn't act like the other two (girl, girls).

    b. That (fox, foxes) ran to the other (foxs, foxes, foxses).

    c. Those (man, mans, men) are following that other (man, mans, men).

    d. My (life, lifes, lives) is like yours. Our (life, lifes, lives) are fun.

    e. This (sheeps, sheep) has thick wool. Those (sheeps, sheep) were shaved.

    f. Those large (babys, babies, baben) cry louder than that small (baby, babie, babies).

The Language Mechanic   Spelling/Vocabulary

YOUR TURN

1. Circle each correct word in parentheses.

   a. One giant (snake, snakes) curled around the two (stick, sticks).

   b. He ate some (snack, snacks) with his (buddys, buddies).

   c. The twin (puppy, puppys, puppies) chased each other around their (mother, mothers).

   d. Five (sheep, sheeps, sheepes) fell asleep. One (sheep, sheeps, sheepes) watched over the rest.

2. In each blank, write the correct plural form of the words *woman, man,* and *child.*

   a. Tell your mother to bring those other _____ along.

   b. That man is following those other _____.

   c. That child is warm, but the other _____ lost their mittens.

3. In each blank, write the correct form of the words *fish* and *deer.*

   When we went fishing, you got one _____. I got two _____.

   One _____ crossed the road. Two other _____ were following.

4. In each blank, write the correct form of *knife.*

   a. Only a sharp _____ cuts well.

   b. Sharpen those dull _____.

5. Underline each plural noun that is written correctly. Cross out and rewrite the ones that are incorrect.

   a. The three foxs jumped.   **d.** He has only two watchs.

   b. They jumped into two boxes.   **e.** The leafs fell from the tree.

   c. I bought all our lunches.   **f.** She ate two loaves of bread.

The Language Mechanic   Spelling/Vocabulary

CHALLENGE

1. In each blank write the word that makes the best sense: *loaf, loafs,* or *loaves.* (Hint: *loaf* can mean to act lazy.)

   a. She baked several _____.

   b. She _____ around in the bakery while eating a _____.

2. Underline the best word in parentheses. (Don't forget: *leave* can be a verb.)

   a. They pick up each (leaf, leave, leaves, leafs).

   b. Then they (leafs, leaves, leave) the yard to put the (leaves, leafs) in a bag.

3. In each blank, use the word that makes the best sense. Write the singular or plural form of each of the following words: *buddy, goody, party, sky, beauty,* and *enemy.*

   The Sun was out and the _____ were clear. We went to a _____

   and ate a lot of _____. My best _____ were there. It was a

   _____ of a day.

Silent Consonants

You want your friend to get more sound out of that bell.

If you write: Wring it some more!

Readers think: He should twist the bell to squeeze the sound out!

You mean: *Ring* it some more!

THE LOGIC

If you leave off a letter, you may be using a word with the wrong meaning. Even a letter that is not pronounced can make a big difference in meaning.

THE RULE

Be sure to include any silent consonants when spelling a word, but don't include letters that don't belong. (Use the list of words with silent consonants on page 142 to help you do the exercises.)

PRACTICE

1. Circle the word in parentheses that makes the best sense.

    If we (wring, ring) that bell, he'll (wring, ring) our necks!

2. In each blank, write the correct word: knight or night.

    a. The _____ grew closer on horseback.

    b. The _____ grew darker as the day ended.

3. Circle the correct word for each sentence.

    a. (Gnat, Nat) swatted a (gnat, nat).

    b. Within an (our, hour) we found (our, hour) way.

    c. I did tie a (not, knot), but he did (not, knot) tie it.

SILENT CONSONANTS: WORD PAIRS

hole/whole
hole: empty pit or pocket
whole: entire

nat/gnat
Nat: a boy's name
gnat: a pesky insect

new/knew
new: not old
knew: past tense form of know

night/knight
night: not daytime
knight: an honored soldier titled "Sir"

not/knot
not: in no way
knot: a fastening of string or cord; to tie

now/know
now: at this time
know: have information

our/hour
our: belonging to us
hour: sixty minutes

ring/wring
ring: make sound as by hitting a bell or to make a circle
wring: squeeze by twisting

rite/write
rite: ceremony
write: put words down

The Language Mechanic   Spelling/Vocabulary

YOUR TURN

1. In each blank, write the number of the matching clue.

   Clue 1: The heat of day nearly killed us.

   Clue 2: One of the king's men helped us.

   a. We were saved by the night. _____

   b. We were saved by the knight. _____

2. In each blank, write the word that makes the most sense: *not/knot, hour/our,* and *whole/hole.*

   a. Do _____ go there, or you'll be tangled in a _____.

   b. You will _____ get out, and you will _____ the rope even more.

   c. They took their lessons, and we took _____ lessons.

   d. They took only 30-minute lessons, but we took _____ lessons.

   e. They dug the _____ ditch.

   f. They dug the _____ deeper.

3. Underline the best word in parentheses.

   She was a (knice, nice) girl. She also (knew, new) her way around in the jungle. She was good at cutting brush with a big (knife, nife). How did she (know, now) how to do that? She had (know, no) training. (Know, Now) she will teach me.

CHALLENGE

1. Underline the word in parentheses that makes the best sense.

   He (writes, rites) about the wedding (writes, rites).

2. Both of the given words could be used in the blank. Discuss why.

   a. He _____ the shirt collar. (wrings, rings)

   b. He would untie the rope, but I would _____. (knot, not)

Silent E for Long Vowels

The Pied Piper is charging more money for getting rid of pests.

If you write: His rats are going up.

Readers think: The mice are climbing high.

You mean: His *rates* are going up.

> **THE LOGIC**
> If you leave the silent *e* off a word with a long vowel sound, the reader may think of a word with a short vowel sound.
>
> **THE RULE**
> When a word has a single vowel before the final consonant, adding an *e* makes the vowel long: *rat*, *rate*.
> • Other words with silent *e* and long vowel sound: *lone, bale, bake, bike, bone*
>
> **SHORT-VOWEL/LONG-VOWEL WORD PAIRS**
> **Can:** 1) a container, 2) be able **Cane:** 1) part of a plant, 2) walking stick
> **Rid:** to do away with **Ride:** to be carried in or by
> **Mat:** a floor pad **Mate:** a helper
> **Win:** to succeed **Wine:** a drink made from grapes
> **Rat:** 1) a rodent, 2) to tell on **Rate:** to judge by a scale

PRACTICE

1. Circle the best word from each pair to complete the sentence.

   a. Get (rid, ride) of that trash. Take it for a (rid, ride).

   b. I (can, cane) see the old man with his (can, cane).

   c. They (win, wine) the best bottle of (win, wine).

   d. The ship's first (mat, mate) was wrestling on the (mat, mate).

The Language Mechanic   Spelling/Vocabulary

YOUR TURN

1. In each blank, write the best word from the list on page 144. Use each word only once.

    a. We _____ on the kids who cheat. We _____ them from one to ten.

    b. Sugar _____ make you sick. Does sugar _____ make you sick?

    c. We _____ the pony. We _____ the pony of pesky flies.

    d. The first _____ took over the ship. The first _____ took years to weave.

    e. Will they _____ the bottle? Will they bottle the _____ ?

2. In each blank, write the number of the matching clue.

    Clue 1: I sunk my teeth into it and got a big chunk.

    Clue 2: I had a tiny piece.

    a. I took a bite of honeycomb. ___   **b.** I took a bit of honeycomb. ___

CHALLENGE

1. Explain why either word could complete the sentence. (Hint: *Fate* means luck or future.)

    a. I depended on (fat, fate) for my survival.

    _____

    b. I wanted a flying toy, so I got a (kit, kite).

    _____

    c. Pick up the (can, cane) of sugar.

    _____

2. Change each word into a new word with a long vowel sound. Write a sentence using the new word: *bit, at, cut, mad, hat, not,* and *sit*. Use another sheet of paper.

Consonant Doubling With -ing or -ed

Your friends and you entered a speech contest. You all wanted to win.

If you write: We all hopped to win the contest.

Readers think: It was a jumping contest.

You mean: We all *hoped* to win the contest.

> **THE LOGIC**
>
> If you leave out the second consonant on a double-consonant word, you may end up with a different word. This may change the meaning of the sentence.
>
> **THE RULE**
>
> When you add *-ed* or *-ing* to a word, use this rule: If the last two letters are a single vowel then a single consonant, double the final consonant: *cap/capped*.
>
> Examples of words ending with a single vowel then a single consonant: *bid, dot, fit, fat, fan, gut, hop, mat, knot, pan, rat, rid, rim, rob, sit, sun, tag, top,* and *whip*.

PRACTICE

1. Circle the words whose last letter should be doubled before adding *-ed* or *-ing*.

   fan   pain   bat   time   sun   rig

2. Circle the best word to complete each sentence.

   a. You should make a (bid, bidd) at the auction. We'll be (biding, bidding) on the vase.

   b. It was (tagged, taged) for selling. We saw the (tagg, tag).

   c. The bids were so low, I thought we were (robing, robbing) the owner.

   d. They (rided, ridded) themselves of that old chair. They are glad to be (rid, ride) of it!

The Language Mechanic   Spelling/Vocabulary

YOUR TURN

1. In each blank, write the number of the matching clue.

   Clue 1: She had headwear.   **Clue 2:** She may not have worn a cap.

   a. A caped woman ran by. _____   **b.** A capped woman ran by. _____

2. Underline the sentences that are written correctly.

   a. He paned for gold.   **b.** He panned for gold.   **c.** He paned the window.

3. Cross out any *-ed* or *-ing* word that is spelled wrong. Write the word correctly.

   He made a cake with whiped cream. It wouldn't fit in the cooler.

   He left it siting in the sun. It was melting. He tried fanning the cake. He could have tried cuting it in two smaller pieces. Instead, he ate the toping.

4. Start with the letters in parentheses to make the best word for each blank. For one blank, double the consonant and add *-ed*. For the other blank, just add *-ed*. (Hint: *waged* means carried on; *fated* means doomed.)

   a. His dog _____ his tail as his owner _____ a war. (wag)

   b. We _____ the calf to make it bigger. It was _____ to be eaten. (fat)

CHALLENGE

1. In each blank, write the number of the matching clue.

   Clue 1: She was coloring a picture.   **Clue 2:** She gave attention to the dog.

   a. She doted on the Dalmatian. _____   **b.** She dotted on the Dalmatian. _____

2. Either given word could complete the sentence. Discuss the difference in meaning for each choice.

   a. They (hated, hatted) her disgusting hairdo.

   b. They win the sack race. They are (hoping, hopping) to get a prize.

UNIT REVIEW: Spelling and Vocabulary

DIRECTIONS: Edit the paragraphs below by crossing out and rewriting the incorrect words.

I am nervous. This will be my first real game of 3-D batball. We are about too play against the Divers, who beet our team last season. The Eagles just *have* to win this time. I can't let them down!

Playing in three dimensions isn't easy. First, you have to be good at floating and gliding. Most people cane do this, but don't no it. Second, you have to be good at bating a ball. The Eagles learned me to put the two skills together. The hole team would hit easy shots to me so I could bate the ball while flying. Then we'd play faster and harder until I was good. That was practice. Now I will play against real players. Mans, woman, and childs will be watching me.

The son shines brightly as the game begins. We play well, cuting the air like knifes as we swoop and turn. We quickly make two goals. Then Callahan, our fastest player, fouls out. She has to set down for the rest of the game! We're down to for players. The Divers catch up by hitting one, then too balls into the goal.

I see a flicker to my left, and I dive four it. False alarm! The ball whizzes by to the write. The Divers get it and take it easily to the goal! I'd better not react so quickly next time. Again, I here the ball whiz by above me. I sea it too late! Sheliah and Jose shake there heads at me in disgust. I almost decide that I'm not cute out for this game. Then the skies darken with clouds, and I grow confident. That's because I usually practice at knight!

I see the ball coming fast. I rays my bat as I eye the goal. May I hit that far? Cory yells, "It's out of bounds! Leave it alone!" I ignore him. I give it all I've got. It flies into the goal! Its just what the Eagles needed to get going. Next, Sheliah slides the ball to Cory right under a Diver's nose and passes it to Jose. He makes another goal! We have become quick and clever like foxs. The Divers have become like sheeps who seem confused and slow.

A Diver is about to pass the ball to her partner. I raise up and surprise her. She almost leaves go of her bat! I pass the ball to Cory, who takes it to the goal. Winning is like taking candy from babys!

The Eagles pat me on the back. "You were great! You were our night in shining armor!" they say. "Thanks, but can I make a suggestion?" I say. We should either practice in the daytime or have our matchs at night!"

GLOSSARY

action verb: (see *verb*)

active voice: (see *voice*)

adjective: a word that tells about a noun (<u>red</u> ball). An adjective is a kind of modifier.

- <u>proper adjective</u>: a specific adjective; a proper adjective must be capitalized (<u>Olympic</u> athlete)

adjective phrase: (see *phrase*)

adverb: a word that tells how, where, or when. An adverb describes a verb, an adjective, or another adverb (he <u>quickly</u> ran, he was <u>very</u> fast, he ran <u>unusually</u> quickly). An adverb is a kind of modifier.

adverb phrase: (see *phrase*)

agreement: having the same number, person, or gender

antecedent: the word a pronoun stands for. In the sentence, "Sue is here because she loves it here" *Sue* is the antecedent of the pronoun *she*.

apostrophe: (see *punctuation*)

appositive: a word or words placed beside another word to explain it. To help you remember "appositive," think of it as being in "a position" by the word(s) it explains.

article: the adjectives *a*, *an*, or *the*. An article is a kind of modifier.

- <u>indefinite article</u>: indefinite articles are *a* and *an*. They are used with general nouns (*a chair, an apple*).

- <u>definite article</u>: The definite article is the word *the*. It is used with specific nouns (*the chair*).

auxiliary verb (helping verb): (see *verb*)

body of friendly letter: (see *letter, friendly*)

capitalize: to make the first letter of a word a capital letter

clause: a group of words that has both a subject and a predicate (whenever he got there OR he got there). A dependent clause cannot be a sentence by itself (whenever he got there). An independent clause can be a sentence by itself but it needs to be capitalized and punctuated (He got there.)

closing of a friendly letter: (see *letter, friendly*)

comma: (see *punctuation*)

common noun: (see *noun*)

comparative: (see *modifier*)

conjunction: a connecting word, such as *and, but,* or *or*

consonant: a letter that is not a vowel (all letters except *a, e, i, o, u;* sometimes *y* is a consonant)

context: the meaning suggested by surrounding words

contraction: the shortened form of a subject and verb (*they'll*) or the shortened form of a verb and the adverb *not (couldn't).* An apostrophe is used to show where letters are left out (see *punctuation: apostrophe*).

definite article: (see *article*)

dependent clause: (see *clause*)

direct quotation: (see *quotation*)

ending punctuation: a mark used to show the end of a sentence. Ending punctuation includes the period, the question mark, and the exclamation mark (see *punctuation*).

exclamation: a statement made forcefully or with strong emotion

exclamation mark: (see *punctuation*)

first person: writing from the "I" point of view.

future tense: (see *verb tense*)

gender: male or female

greeting of a friendly letter: (see *letter, friendly*)

helping verb: (see *verb: auxiliary verb*)

homophones: words that sound the same, but have different meanings and, often, different spellings

indefinite article: (see *article*)

independent clause: (see *clause*)

indirect quotation: (see *quotation*)

interjection: a simple exclamation or an interruption; a strong interjection should be followed by an exclamation mark (*Hah! Mercy! Oops!*)

introductory word: A word that begins a sentence and introduces the rest of the sentence; it is separated from the rest of the sentence with a comma.

introductory dependent clause: A dependent clause that is before the independent main clause; a comma must be placed after an introductory dependent clause.

irregular verb: (see *verb*)

letter, friendly:

- body: the main part of the letter, between the greeting and the closing
- closing: a modifier and noun used to close the letter; both are capitalized and separated by a comma (*Sincerely, Gertrude*)
- greeting of a friendly letter: the adjective and noun that introduce the body of a letter, followed by a comma (*Dear Haley,*)

linking verb: (see *verb*)

logic: reasoning, or making sense

misplaced modifier: a modifier that is not close enough to the word(s) it tells about. It seems to tell about the wrong word.

modifier: an adjective or adverb; a word that describes another word or changes its meaning. Articles are really adjectives, so the words *a*, *an*, and *the* are modifiers, too.

- positive: the basic form of adjective or adverb, showing no comparison (large, quiet, beautiful)
- comparative: the degree of comparison meaning more in some way (larger, quieter, more beautiful)
- superlative: a degree of comparison meaning *most* in some way (largest, quickest, most beautiful)

negative: a word that changes another word's meaning to its opposite. *Not going* means the opposite of *going*. (not, no, hardly, scarcely are negatives)

noun of address: the name of the person being spoken to (addressed)

noun: a word for a person, place, or thing

- common noun: a word for a general noun. A common noun is not capitalized (unless it begins a sentence).
- gender: whether a noun is male or female
- proper noun: the name for a particular person, place, or thing. A proper noun should be capitalized.
- possessive noun: a noun that shows ownership (*Ned's* bike, a *boy's* watch)
- person: shows the noun's relationship to the speaker (or writer). First person is *I, me, we,* or *us*; second person is *you*; third person is *he, she, it,* or *they.*
- number: whether a noun is singular or plural. This noun and verb are singular in number: *boy runs*. This noun and verb are plural in number: *boys run.* The letter *s* can show that a noun is plural, but *s* can also show that a verb is singular! (see also *singular, plural*)

object: (see *subject/object*)

parallel tense: (see *verb tense*)

parentheses: (see *punctuation: parentheses*)

passive voice: (see *voice: passive* voice)

past tense: (see *verb tense*)

person: (see *noun*)

phrase: a group of words that work together. The phrase acts as a part of speech and does not have a subject and predicate. The words *his father* may act as subject or object. The words *in the dark* may act as an adverb or adjective.

- adjective phrase: any phrase which modifies a noun or pronoun.
- adverb phrase: a prepositional phrase that functions as an adverb.

plain verb: (see *verb*)

plural: the number of a noun or verb showing that there is more than one (see also *noun: number*)

positive modifier: (see *modifier*)

possessive noun or pronoun: (see *noun* and *pronoun*)

present tense: (see *verb tense*)

pronoun: a word that stands for a noun (*he can* stand for Ned, *they* can stand for Bob and Alice, etc.)

- possessive pronoun: a pronoun showing ownership (*my* bike, *yours*, *ours*, *his* house)

proper adjective: (see *adjective*)

proper noun: (see *noun*)

punctuation:

- apostrophe: ' An apostrophe is used to stand for letters in a *contraction* (*don't*) and to show ownership in *possessive* words (*Rudolf's*).
- comma: , A comma is used to separate ideas.
- period: . A period is used to end a statement.
- question mark: ? A question mark is used at the end of a question sentence.
- quotation marks: " " Quotation marks are used on either side of the exact words that were spoken or of the words in a title.
- parentheses: ( ) curves used to enclose extra information (these words are between two parentheses).

- exclamation marks: ! An exclamation mark is used to end a strong statement.

question: a sentence that asks something. A question ends with a question mark.

question mark: (see *punctuation*)

quotation:

- direct quotation: the exact words spoken by someone. A direct quotation should be enclosed in quotation marks (He said, "I like you!").
- indirect quotation: words about what was said. An indirect quotation needs no quotation marks (He told me he liked me.)
- split quotation: a direct quotation that is divided or interrupted. Both parts should be enclosed in quotation marks. "I like you," he said, "because you're nice."

quotation marks: (see *punctuation*)

regular verb: (see *verb*)

run-on: placed together without correct words, capitalization, or punctuation to separate different ideas. A run-on sentence needs to be separated into more than one sentence. Each sentence should be a clear, complete thought.

sentence: words that show a complete thought. The first word of a sentence is capitalized. A sentence has ending punctuation such as a period, question mark, or exlamation mark. (see also *run-on*)

series, words in a series: a list of similar words, phrases, or clauses; words in a series should be separated by commas. (*We mended clothes, put them on, and went out.*)

singular: the number of a noun or verb showing that there is only one (see also *noun: number*)

split quotation: (see *quotation*)

subject/object:

- subject: a word or words for who or what the sentence is about
- object: the receiver of the verb's action (He threw *the ball.*)

superlative: (see *modifier: comparative forms*)

syllable: a division of a word. The word *wonderful* is spoken in three parts, or syllables: *won-der-ful.*

tense: (see *verb: tense*)

verb: a word that shows action or state of being (condition)

- action verb: a verb that shows action
- linking verb: a verb that shows the condition of the subject. The linking verb joins the subject to another word (he *looks* happy). If a verb is a linking verb, it can be replaced with a form of the verb *to be* so that the sentence still makes sense (he *is* happy).
- auxiliary verb (helping verb): the part of the verb that comes before the main verb (*am* going)
- regular verb: a verb that follows the regular rules for forming tense (the past tense is formed by adding *ed* to the plain verb).
- irregular verb: a verb that does not follow the regular rules for forming tense. The verb *teach* is irregular. The past tense is *taught*, not *teached*.
- plain verb: the common verb form
- tense: the verb form that shows when an action occurred, occurs, or will occur (past, present, future). See *verb tense*.

verb tense:

- future tense: a verb form showing that an action will take place after now
- past tense: the verb form showing that an action took place before now
- present tense: the verb form showing that an action takes place now (present time)
- parallel tense: having similar verb form (all past, all present, or all future)

voice: the form of the verb that shows how strong the subject is

- active voice: shows that the subject does the acting: He throws the ball.
- passive voice: shows that the subject is acted upon: He was thrown.

vowel: the letters *a, e, i, o,* or *u* (and sometimes *y*)

ANSWER KEY

UNIT 1: CAPITALIZATION
Proper Nouns: Names of People
PRACTICE **(pg. 1)**
1. Answers will vary **2a.** 1 **2b.** 2
CHART **(pg. 2)** Answers will vary
YOUR TURN **(pg. 3)**
1a. 2 **1b.** 1 **1c.** 2 **1d.** 1
2a. stretch **2b.** Stretch
3. Hello, solon. This woman's name is smoky. She is our club president. Please show president smoky where my mom is sitting. I know dad would love to meet her, too.
CHALLENGE **(pg. 4)**
1a. President **1b.** president
2. b. I think the letters g and h were there, but i was not sure.
3. A road that is long could be called a long stretch because it stretches out far. The road is also a long Stretch, because Stretch is its name.

Proper Nouns: Name of Places and Things
PRACTICE **(pg. 5)**
1. Answers will vary **2.** Texas, Florida, November, January, Italy, Tower of Pisa, St. Paul's Cathedral, Hampton College **3a.** China **3b.** china
YOUR TURN **(pg. 6)**
1a. 2 **1b.** 1
2a. major storm **2b.** Major Storm
3. Sunday, Friday (Sunday and Friday are names of days of the week.)
4a. north pole, North Pole **4b.** pleasant times, Pleasant Times **4c.** dance up a storm, Dance Up a Storm **4d.** all fired up, All Fired Up
CHALLENGE **(pg. 7)**
1a. 1 **1b.** 2
2a. March **2b.** July
3. Thursday, Groundhog day (Thursday is a day of the week; Groundhog Day is a holiday.)

Proper Adjectives
PRACTICE **(pg. 8)**
1. Answers will vary **2a.** Martian (battle)
2b. Goodwill (store) **3.** b
CHART **(pg. 9)** Answers will vary

YOUR TURN **(pg. 10)**
1a. 1 **1b.** 2
2a. (student's birth month, capitalized)
2b. (student's state, capitalized)
3a. Hawaiian **3b.** June, May
CHALLENGE **(pg. 10)**
1a. july, july **1b.** fourth of july

UNIT REVIEW: Capitalization (pg. 11)
Monday, June, Ratland, I, Catzilla, Statue of Liberty, Rattan, Mousetrap, September, Principal Ryan, French, Rodent Run College, Ratland, Mousa Lisa, Home on the Mousepad

UNIT 2: RUN-ONS AND FRAGMENTS
Run-On Sentences
PRACTICE **(pg. 12)**
1b. works. **1c.** noon. When **2a.** energy. He
2b. pain. That **2c.** leave sentence as is
YOUR TURN **(pg. 13)**
1b. around. The **1c.** town. She **1d.** car. We
1e. drive. It
2. c
3. b
CHALLENGE **(pg. 14)**
1a. fish. We **1b.** monsters. We **1c.** come. On
1d. Wednesday. I
2. shoe. The
3a. 1 **3b.** 2

Interjections
PRACTICE **(pg. 15)**
1a. I see the tower. Wow! It's huge. **1b.** She snubbed me. Well! That's rude. **2.** (b)
YOUR TURN **(pg. 16)**
1a. Rats! I **1b.** Cool! I **1c.** lunch. Oops!
1d. Well! I
2a. players? Great! We
2b. picnic. I brought two dozen. Rats! I
3a. 1 **3b.** 2 **3c.** 2 **3d.** 1
CHALLENGE **(pg. 17)**
1a. clothes? Darn! I wish you would. Those holey socks show my toes. **1b.** clothes? I wish you would darn those holy socks that show my toes.

The Language Mechanic — Answer Key

2. Oh! I dropped my ring. It's hiding under the chair. Can I reach it? Yikes! A spider is on my finger. I'll try again. Ouch! I burned my hand on the heater. Now I've got it. Cool!
(If you wrote "Now I've got it cool," it would mean you got your hand cool after burning it. When you separate "Cool" as an interjection, it means everything's fine!)

Direct Quotations
PRACTICE (pg. 18)
1. b 2a. "Go away," he snarled. 2b. "Is it time?" she asked. "We are ready to go."
2c. "Here she comes," he said, "whether we like it or not."
YOUR TURN (pg. 19)
1a. "Let's 1b. "Let's go in," he said, "when it rains."
2. b (The clue says you had no tears, so *a* must be wrong.)
3a. She said there were seven dogs.
3b. She said, "There were seven dogs."
3c. The new boy asked, "Where is the lunchroom?" Jo said, "It's in the basement."
3d. "Give him an inch," she said, "and he'll take a mile."
4a. 2 4b. 1
CHALLENGE (pg. 20)
1a. 1 1b. 3 1c. 2 (1 is also acceptable for choice c, however the directions limit you to using each clue only once.)
2a. 2 2b. 1
3. I heard you cried, John.
   I heard you cried, "John!"
   "I heard you!" cried John.
   "I heard you cried, John."

Sentence Fragments
PRACTICE (pg. 21)
1a. He had fun building his robot. 1b. He added a switch to make the eyes move. 2. b
YOUR TURN (pg. 22)
1. We had fun at the fair. My parents drove us in the car. Were you and your friend there? The roller coaster went so fast that my hat flew off!
2. b
3. He writes letters with a pen. He draws pictures.

CHALLENGE (pg. 22)
1. We saw the reindeer. Is fishing your favorite sport?
2a. They designed the building in 1955. We built it.
2b. They designed the building. In 1955, we built it.

UNIT REVIEW: Run-Ons and Fragments (pg. 23)
We decided to start a school for pets. Who would come? Cats, dogs, and gerbils would attend. Even snakes might be welcome. What would we teach? Mrs. Jocer asked, "Could you teach my snake to hop like a toad?" We said, "Of course we could." Dr. Jones asked if we could teach his cat to slither. "No problem," we said. "Could you teach my dog," Ms. Forster asked, "to bark like a dog?" We said, " Sure."
We began our work. Rats! The cat kept running. The dog kept sitting quietly. The snake kept slithering. Then something weird happened. The cat and snake became friends. The cat slithered. The snake tried to copy the cat. It couldn't run. It sprang up and fell back again and again. The dog was so surprised that it started to bark. The owners came back. Dr. Jones was very happy to see his slithering cat. Ms. Forster was thrilled to hear her dog bark. Mrs. Jocer saw her snake. She said, "That's the best toad hopping I've ever seen."
They all said we were great. Teachers like us are hard to find, I guess.

UNIT 3: PRONOUNS
Pronoun as Subject and Object
PRACTICE (pg. 24)
1. Subjects: I, he, she, they, we, you. Objects: me, him, us, them, her, you. 2a. she, them
2b. I 2c. me
YOUR TURN (pg. 25)
1a. us 1b. We 1c. He 1d. them
2a. We 2b. them
3a. We 3b. us
4a. 1 4b. 2
5. Come with us smart people. You and we will join the mighty Wookajigs. You can see them staring at us.
CHALLENGE (pg. 26)
1a. 2 1b. 1
2a. I can jump higher than the hurdles. 2b. I can

jump higher than my two friends can jump.

Possessive Pronouns
PRACTICE (pg. 27)
1a. your **1b.** my **1c.** their **1d.** ours **2a.** 2 **2b.** 1
YOUR TURN (pg. 28)
1a. Mine, yours, Its **1b.** your, my, mine, yours
2a. 1 **2b.** 2
3. Answers will vary (Example: **3a.** his head **3b.** our team **3c.** theirs)
CHALLENGE (pg. 28)
1a. ii **1b.** i
2a. 1 **2b.** 2

First Person Last
PRACTICE (pg. 29)
1. ⓑ **2a.** He and I **2b.** her and me **2c.** They and we **2d.** them and us
YOUR TURN (pg. 30)
1. ⓑ and ⓒ
2a. Mom and I **2b.** Sis and me **2c.** them and us **2d.** they and we
3a. John, Lester, and I **3b.** Rula, Cappy, and me
4. Maybe they will find them and us! Maybe my brother and we will bury some coins. The kids and grownups will find them. (OR reverse, order doesn't matter)
CHALLENGE (pg. 30)
1. They and we will all look at pictures of Clarence, you, Dad, and me.

UNIT REVIEW Pronouns (pg. 31)
PET SWAP
Sister and Brother and I all had pets. He had a cat that she liked. I said he should give her his cat. Sister would then give her dog to me. Then I would let him have my raptor. I would take the monkey and gerbil from him and her. Brother would then share my mongoose with her. They and I would be as happy as clams.
DANGER ON MARS
Gerard and I spent two days on Mars without food. Our folks had given him and me a hundred dronchoks each. It had been a rough landing in our Planet Rover. We thought the MarCats would repair the Rover. Instead, they took both his money and mine. They and we were now enemies. We wanted to put distance between them and us. Gerard and I were now in danger. It looked bad for him and me. I knew others had survived their Mars journey. We would just have to live through ours, too.

UNIT 4: MODIFIERS
Using Adjectives and Adverbs
PRACTICE (pg. 32)
1a. scratchy, sharp **1b.** deep, shallow **2.** Answers will vary (Examples: **2a.** fast, slow, speedy
2b. red, green **2c.** small, large, big **2d.** cheap, inexpensive)
PRACTICE II (pg. 33)
a. slowly **b.** carefully **c.** lightly **d.** clumsily
e. badly (or poorly)
PRACTICE III (pg. 33)
1c. 2 **1d.** 1 **2a.** adjective **2b.** adjective
2c. adverb
YOUR TURN (pg. 34)
1a. slowly, slow **1b.** sad, sadly
2a. 2 **2b.** 1 **2c.** 1 **2d.** 2
3a. smooth **3b.** roughly
4a. 2 **4b.** 1
CHALLENGE (pg. 35)
1a. 1 **1b.** 2
2b. He has a pleasant fragrance. **2c.** They look healthy (or they are thorough about looking for something).

Comparative/Superlative Modifiers
PRACTICE (pg. 36)
1a. some, more, most **1b.** fastest **1c.** faster
YOUR TURN (pg. 37)
1a. taller **1b.** tallest
2a. worst, best **2b.** better
3a. more, the most **3b.** less **3c.** stronger
3d. liveliest
CHALLENGE (pg. 37)
1a. two **1b.** three **1c.** most dependable **1d.** more dependable
2. ⓐ, ⓓ

Articles: A, An
PRACTICE (pg. 38)
1. incorrect: a, d **2a.** 1 **2b.** 2

YOUR TURN (pg. 39)
1. Incorrect: b, c, d
2a. fishy 2b. a bird
3a. 1 3b. 2 3c. 1 3d. 2
CHALLENGE (pg. 39)
1a. 1 1b. 2 1c. 1 1d. 2
2a. 2 2b. 1

Articles: A and The With General & Specific Nouns
PRACTICE (pg. 40)
1a. The 1b. A 2a. 2 2b. 1
YOUR TURN (pg. 41)
1. The, a, the
2a. a 2b. the
3a. the 3b. a
4a. 1 4b. 2
CHALLENGE (pg. 41)
1. The, A, The, The (If 3 bubbles of 5 were medium sized, there must have been one larger and one smaller.)
2a. 1 2b. 2
3. ⓐ

Misplaced Modifiers
PRACTICE (pg. 42)
1. Cross out: a, c 2a. 1 2b. 2 2c. 2
YOUR TURN (pg. 43)
1. Incorrect: a, d
2a. 2 2b. 1 2c. 1 2d. 2
3b. The girl giving her speech held up the toad.
3c. The people throwing snowballs watched the reindeer.
CHALLENGE (pg. 44)
1a. bunnies 1b. boys
2a. hopping, quickly, small
2b. spotted, slowly, tall

UNIT REVIEW: Modifiers (pg. 45)
1. I was excited about leaving San Jose! There were two flights to Ottawa. I would take the earlier one then change planes in Chicago. That's why I got up at 5:00 A.M. A sleeping boy can't catch an early plane!
2. The large flight would take off at 6:00. A sign said the flight would be late! I would have to wait an hour longer. I ate an egg. I read a comic book. At 6:45, we boarded the plane. At last! I quickly fastened my long seatbelt so it was tight.
3. The pilot said Chicago had snowstorms. We would have to wait another whole hour to go! It seemed like the longest hour in my life. What would I do? I had one game and two books. I played the only game I had. I read a book. Later, I'd read the other one. My right hand was sore, so I held the book with my weaker hand.
4. Finally, we took off. An airplane can fly very smoothly. This was a smooth flight at first. Then it got rough. I looked at the couple in the next seat. The snoring man missed the excitement. The shaking woman tried to watch the movie. She was the more nervous of those two.
5. After awhile, the weather got better. The sun shone more brightly than before. The clouds were whiter than ever. I was the happiest of all passengers.

UNIT 5: VERBS
Past, Present, and Future Tense
PRACTICE (pg. 46)
1. learned, learn, will learn 2. 1 hope, 2 wait, 3 eat
YOUR TURN (pg. 47)
1b. will enjoy 1c. played 1d. whispered
1e. will finish 1f. looks
2. will open, missed, untie
CHALLENGE (pg. 47)
1. gaze (Pr), showed (P), move (Pr), will look (F), will change (F), appeared (P)

Irregular Verb Forms
PRACTICE (pg. 48)
1. take, took, will take 2a. 1 2b. 3 2c. 4 2d. 2
YOUR TURN (pg. 50)
1a. drove 1b. drew 1c. fell
2a. The dove flew down the chimney flue.
2b. We rode along the path as they rode on the road.
2c. Only one branch had leaved, so we left to find a park with nicer trees.
2d. We read the book as he read the paper.
2e. She did the dishes with a handsome dude.
3a. 1 3b. 2 3c. 3

CHALLENGE (pg. 50)
1. stole (replaces *stealed*)
2a. *They halved the cake* is correct because it means they cut it in halves. *They had the cake* is correct because it means they ate it.
2b. *The girl saw a log* can be correct because she could have seen it with her eyes. *The girl sawed a log* could be correct because she might have used a saw to cut the log.

Parallel Construction for Tense
PRACTICE (pg. 51)
1a. ⓒ **2a.** Either change *ate* to *eat*, or change *find* to *found*. **2b.** Either change *Did* to *Do* or change the second *do* to *did*.
YOUR TURN (pg. 52)
1. walked, picked
2a. was **2b.** took **2c.** turns
3a. will play **3b.** eat, will eat
CHALLENGE (pg. 52)
1. ⓐ,ⓒ
2. ⓑ

Helping Verbs
PRACTICE (pg. 53)
1a. was **1b.** am **1c.** has **1d.** did **2a.** 1, 3
2b. 2, 3
YOUR TURN (pg. 54)
1a. have, were **1b.** must, will
2a. was, did **2b.** are, should
3. He <u>could</u> not read them without his glasses. I <u>am</u> going to the race tomorrow. Maybe I <u>should</u> get some sleep.
4a. 1 **4b.** 2 (The reason 2 is best for *b* is that *did* helps emphasize the answer.)
5a. will, can **5b.** have, had
CHALLENGE (pg. 54)
1a. How far we run! **1b.** How far can we run?
2a. The helper *am* means that I am not the one who painted. Someone painted me.
2b. The helper *will* means that we are not now running, but will run later.

Linking Verbs
PRACTICE (pg. 55)
1a. taste **1b.** look **1c.** are **2a.** Underline the second *look* **2b.** Underline the first *grown*

YOUR TURN (pg. 56)
1. looked, smelled, felt
2a. It <u>sounded</u> full. I <u>grew</u> tired, but it finally broke! It <u>tasted</u> very sweet.
3. are, looks, seem, grow, is
CHALLENGE (pg. 56)
1a. A, L **1b.** L, A **1c.** L, A

UNIT REVIEW: Verbs (pg. 57)
A: Elena was new. My friends and I <u>made</u> fun as she walked into the classroom. Her hair was a stringy mess that covered her eyes. Her shoes were two sizes too big, and they <u>were</u> scuffed. Her socks didn't even match! How could she be so careless? When Dory said, "Hi, Rags," we <u>laughed</u> out loud. I know Elena <u>heard</u> us, but I <u>couldn't</u> help it. Anyway, she <u>deserved</u> it. She could have paid more attention to her clothes. When she passed us, she even <u>smelled</u> bad. She <u>hung</u> her head down. She bumped into a desk and <u>ran</u> off. Couldn't she even watch where she was going? I <u>forgot</u> about her until that night.
B: The phone rang after dinner. Mom <u>talked</u> with her best friend, Alice, for awhile. Then Mom <u>said</u>, "No problem. She can stay here in Marcy's room." She <u>hung</u> up and said, "Alice's relatives <u>lost</u> their house in a fire. They stayed with Alice last night, but it was crowded. The kids have no decent clothes. Alice will find them some tomorrow. Maybe you could loan the girl some of your things, Marcy. She will be over in a few minutes. I <u>felt</u> sorry for the girl, but I was not ready for what I saw at the door. My mouth <u>fell</u> open. All I <u>could</u> say was "You?" It was Elena! She <u>acted</u> as surprised as I.
C: Suddenly I felt ashamed. No wonder she <u>wore</u> shoes that were too big. No wonder she had no time or help to fix her hair. How would I feel if I <u>had</u> to go to school like that?
D: "I didn't know about your house, Elena. I was mean and I'm sorry," I apologized. It <u>took</u> her awhile to trust me. I loaned her some nice clothes and <u>made</u> her feel at home. She turned out to be really fun! I decided to introduce her to my friends. I <u>swore</u> I would never make fun of anyone again. There may always be a hidden reason for the things people do.

UNIT 6: AGREEMENT

Pronoun/Antecedent Agree in Gender
PRACTICE (pg. 58)
1a. She **2a.** He **2b.** She
YOUR TURN (pg. 59)
1a. he **1b.** She **1c.** he **1d.** he
2a. She (Since Jake is always calm, it can't be "he.") **2b.** He, she
3a. 1 **3b.** 2
CHALLENGE (pg. 60)
1a. She ran and told the ram. He was glad to hear her news.
1b. He told her to load her bike into his SUV. He would drive her and her bike to the lake. Then he would help her unload.
She would speed through the mountain roads on her two wheels. Meanwhile, he would stay at the lake in his dark vehicle.
2. Valerie owned Jonny, the male cat. Bob owned Sylvia, the female dog. When they got her cat ready to go the vet, his dog got upset. She wanted to go, too. Mom drove them both in her new car. When she took Jonny in to get his shot, Sylvia went with her. As soon as they entered the office, Sylvia changed her mind. She no longer wanted to be there. Jonny was a brave cat. He had done this many times. He sat waiting patiently while the dog struggled to get off her leash and out the door.

Pronoun/Antecedent Agree in Number
PRACTICE (pg. 61)
1a. his, it **1b.** they **2a.** They were **2b.** It was
YOUR TURN (pg. 62)
1a. they were **1b.** it **1c.** it was **1d.** they were
2a. his **2b.** her **2c.** their **2d.** its
3a. them **3b.** them
4a. his **4b.** their
CHALLENGE (pg. 62)
1a. They **1b.** it
2. Several objects glided through space. First was a slender steel spoon. Behind it was a green and purple stuffed snake. A rubber duck followed. They were all moving toward a strange planet. This planet sucked all the objects from space. It was like a vacuum cleaner for objects. They stuck to the planet like the tape.

Noun or Pronoun/Verb Agree in Number
PRACTICE (pg. 63)
1a. leaps **1b.** lie **2.** He or she has chocolate kisses. You have jelly beans. These are better than those.
YOUR TURN (pg. 64)
1a. are **1b.** They **1c.** looks **1d.** Mr. Hensley and Ms. White **1e.** He
2a. finds **2b.** go **2c.** drive **2d.** rent **2e.** runs
2f. looks **2g.** laughs **2h.** have **2i.** walks **2j.** eat
3a. does **3b.** run **3c.** leaps **3d.** swim **3e.** eats
CHALLENGE (pg. 65)
1a. are, them **1b.** is, it
2. is, is, are, is
3. The pirates of third grade look fierce. Tam and Mark look tough. They both wear eye patches. Two of the girls have parrots on their shoulders. The parrots sing, and they squawk loudly. Do not be afraid. These kids are good pirates. They help kids who are being picked on. The pirates yell at the bullies and chase them away.

Adjective/Noun Agree in Number
PRACTICE (pg. 66)
1a. some bats, one glove **1b.** this game, these parks **1c.** that necklace, those dresses **2a.** these, this **3a.** those, that
YOUR TURN (pg. 67)
1a. any, some **1b.** one, all **1c.** This, these **1d.** these, this
2b. one (S), several (P), eleven (P)
2c. many (P), this (S), those (P)
CHALLENGE (pg. 67)
1a. Answers will vary (Example: Those, That)
1b. Answers will vary (Example: One, Three)
2. He showed me some maps. One map showed only one park. I said, "I'll take this map." Then I found all of those parks.

Adjectives (This, That)/Noun Agree in Space or Time
PRACTICE (pg. 68)
1a. That, This **1b.** These, those **2.** this, that
YOUR TURN (pg. 69)
1a. those, these **1b.** those, these
2a. big **2b.** small **2c.** red **2d.** blue
3a. That, this **3b.** That, this

4a. This (The clue is in the tense *is*. *That* could be accepted if student personifies the months, as when we look at schedules for several months at a time and say "This one is busy, but that one is not."), That
4b. That, This
CHALLENGE (pg. 70)
1a. that, this **1b.** this, that
2a. left **2b.** right **2c.** left **2d.** right
3. I found 28 red and orange gummy slugs here on the table. He found 32 gray ones there on the floor. These slugs are more colorful than those slugs. I would rather look in this spot. I think that spot is dirtier. Put these 28 slugs in the candy dish. Put those 32 slugs in the trash. Tomorrow we will have another gummy hunt. That hunt may give us one hundred good slugs. This hunt gave us only 28 good ones.

UNIT REVIEW: Agreement (pg. 71)
We live by a beach resort. Mr. Wiggle has our surfboards over at his house. Gin and I have our snowboards at our house. These boards are for the resort in the mountains. We'll use these other boards when we go to our beach. This week, we will go to that mountain resort because it has snow. Next week, we'll come back to this beach resort because it is great for surfing.
One time we were skiing, Gin hit a bump, and she fell on her face. I laughed so hard I got a stomachache. I was so busy laughing, I slowly glided into a tree! Now, Gin laughs at me when she remembers that day.
We have our laughs at the beach, too. One time, Arnold picked up a board that wasn't his own. He didn't notice his mistake until a boy yelled, "Thief!" Boy, was Arnold's face red! He gave it back and said he was sorry. The two boys shook hands. Now they are friends.

UNIT 7: UNNECESSARY WORDS
Double Negatives
PRACTICE (pg. 72)
1. ⓑ, ⓒ **2.** ⓑ
YOUR TURN (pg. 73)
1. ⓑ, ⓒ
2. ⓓ

3a. There's hardly any rain.
3b. We scarcely ever have fun. (OR We never have fun. OR We scarcely have any rain.)
4. ⓐ, ⓑ, ⓓ
CHALLENGE (pg. 73)
1a. 2 **1b.** 1
2a. Do it. **2b.** Somebody is in there.

Noun or Pronoun (Not Both) As Subject
PRACTICE (pg. 74)
1a. 1 **1b.** 3 **1c.** 2   **2.** Only b makes sense. In both a and c, cross out the word *it*.
YOUR TURN (pg. 75)
1a. The ice ~~it~~ is cold. **1b.** The boy ~~he~~ won't behave.
2a. When the ice skate ~~it~~ is cold, his foot ~~it~~ won't go in.
2b. The swooshing Snarfo ~~he~~ dives into the mud.
3. Terrence ~~he~~ goes to college. The college ~~it~~ is beautiful. People ~~they~~ hike the trail often.
4a. Cindy ~~she~~ puts on her sneakers. Then ~~Cindy~~ she walks 5 miles.
4b. Rosco loves music, and ~~Rosco's~~ his favorite music is jazz.
CHALLENGE (pg. 75)
1a. 2 **1b.** 1
2. Line *a* means when they ride bulls, they are happy; line *b* means running bulls are scary.

Here/There With This/That
PRACTICE (pg. 76)
1. ⓑ **2.** cross out: *b*
YOUR TURN (pg. 77)
1. ⓒ
2. This ~~here~~ tiger is huge. Those ~~there~~ jaws are strong. What if he runs over here? Use that ~~there~~ stick to scare him away. Seeing the tiger over there is better than having the tiger here. We enjoy him from this ~~here~~ spot.
3. a
4. Take that ~~there~~ teddy bear off the carpet.
CHALLENGE (pg. 77)
1a. 2 **1b.** 3 **1c.** 1
2. As is, you are asking if the train is here on time. If you are asking whether the train that is here is on time, say either "Is this train on time?" OR "Is the train that is here on time?"

UNIT REVIEW: Unnecessary Words (pg. 78)
Nobody ~~can't~~ can see the game from here!" wails Jenny. Jenny ~~she~~ is right. These ~~here~~ seats are too high in the stands. The players don't look ~~no~~ any bigger than ants. Jenny and I ~~we~~ look for better seats. There is hardly ~~nothing~~ anything left empty. (OR There are hardly any left empty.) I say, "Hold this ~~here~~ drink. Keep this sandwich here too." Then I see that ~~there~~ woman at the exit. I say, "Jen, she looks like she's leaving." I run over there. I ask if she's leaving.
She says, "My son ~~he~~ ate too much and doesn't feel ~~no~~ good. We've scarcely ~~never~~ ever been to a game."
I say, "I came with my sister. We can't see from our seats. Do you mind if we use those ~~there~~ seats of yours?"
She says, "No, ~~Jake and I~~ we're not coming back. Have fun."
The day ends for the playmates. Rat ~~he~~ scampers home. Char ~~she~~ walks lazily by the river. The trees ~~they~~ grow so tall. Her purse ~~it~~ feels so heavy. Near her, people ~~they~~ lie on the ground. She decides to lie down too.

UNIT 8: PUNCTUATION ' ? ! " "
Apostrophe: Contractions
PRACTICE (pg. 79)
1a. aren't **1b.** I'll **1c.** You've **1d.** She's
1e. can't **1f.** You'll **2a.** we're **2b.** were
YOUR TURN (pg. 80)
1a. we've **1b.** weave
2. b **3a.** We've, they'd **3b.** She'll **3c.** They're
3d. wouldn't
4a. 1 (In this case *car's* means car has) **4b.** 2
CHALLENGE (pg. 81)
1a. it's (it is) **1b.** its
2a. ~~Their~~ They're **2b.** ~~whose~~ who's
3a. In the first sentence, *were* is a verb that goes with the subject *They* (They were always there). In the second sentence, *we're* means we are (we are always there).
3b. In the first sentence, *roads* is a plural and the sentence asks if you know those roads in the area. In the second sentence, *road's* means road is, and you are asked if you know that the road is surrounding you.

4. It would say I'd rather *wed*, meaning I'd rather get married!

Apostrophe With Singular Possessive
PRACTICE (pg. 82)
1a. Bob's books **1b.** book's cover **1c.** girl's bag
2a. friend's **2b.** friends
YOUR TURN (pg. 83)
1a. man's **1b.** woman's **1c.** child's
2a. The first sentence is correct: The bear's paw has a thorn.
2b. The second sentence is correct: They go with Nettie's aunts.
3. leader's, baby's, woman's, child's, man's
4. Answers will vary (Examples: **4b.** the principal's **4c.** my mother's **4d.** sister's
4e. school's
CHALLENGE (pg. 84)
1a. There was one bird nest in the tree. (We saw the bird's nest in the tree.)
1b. There was more than one bird nesting in the tree. (We saw the birds nest in the tree.)
2a. 1 **2b.** 2 **2c.** 2 **2d.** 1 **2e.** 2 **2f.** 1

Apostrophe With Plural Possessive
PRACTICE (pg. 85)
1. foxes', babies', adults', fathers' **2.** men's, children's, people's, deer's **3.** a and d
YOUR TURN (pg. 86)
1a. Those books' covers are dirty.
1b. Those girls' cases look heavy. I met the two sisters' father.
1c. Put the children's coats on the children.
1d. We women saw the other women's team yesterday.
2a. P **2b.** S **2c.** S **2d.** P
3. a
4a. women's **4b.** woman's **4c.** Children's
4d. child's
5a. friends' **5b.** dogs'
6. doors', door's, doors
CHALLENGE (pg. 87)
1a. N **1b.** V
2a. The girls are sealing the leaks.
2b. One girl has a seal that leaks.
2c. More than one girl have a seal that leaks.

3. Clue 1: a Clue 2: c
Statement *a* means that more than one worker changes ends of something. Statement *b* means that the work period of more than one worker ends. Statement *c* means that the work period of one worker ends.

Question Mark
PRACTICE (pg. 88)
1a. 2 **1b.** 1 **2a.** hear. **2b.** hear? **3a.** today?
3b. today. **3c.** sing. **3d.** sing?
YOUR TURN (pg. 89)
1a. chocolate? chocolate. **1b.** going? going.
1c. sister. brother? **1d.** pet. shirt?
2a. 2 **2b.** 1 **2c.** 1 **2d.** 2
3a. weary? **3b.** works? **3c.** hard. **3d.** sleeps?
3e. here? **3f.** sleeps.
CHALLENGE (pg. 89)
1a. that? **1b.** that! (question mark is possible, but it is likely that the owner of the sneakers is angry rather than curious.) **1c.** it? I!
2a. are? are. **2b.** diary?

Exclamation Mark
PRACTICE (pg. 90)
1a. it! **1b.** okay. (Mark is not too excited.)
2a. wow. impressed. **2b.** wow! impressed!
YOUR TURN (pg. 91)
1a. peas! **1b.** ship! **1c.** ride.
2a. D **2b.** C **2c.** A **2d.** B
3a. bandages! **3b.** chair. **3c.** way! **3d.** lottery!
3e. tomorrow. **3f.** that!
CHALLENGE (pg. 91)
1. Joey: awesome! great! **Jill**: ride! SWOOSH!
2a. sit? **2b.** movie!

Quotation Marks
PRACTICE (pg. 92)
1a. "The Hero" **1b.** "Blue Ice" **2a.** the first "The Tree" **2b.** the second "Bonnie" **3a.** 1
3b. 2
YOUR TURN (pg. 93)
1a. "Bright Patch." **1b.** "Brice's Canyon"
2a. They enjoyed "New York" **2b.** "Papa"
2c. "David"
3a. 2 **3b.** 1

CHALLENGE (pg. 93)
1. "Dazed Dolphin" "Harold and Maude"
2a. "Butterflies" is enjoyable to hear.
2b. "Grandparents" is fun to watch.

UNIT REVIEW: Punctuation (pg. 94)
Bobby's Bonita's children's (*school?* is correct as is) museum. Let's I'd minutes?" I'll finds kittens' "Men's" "Yikes!" "Hay Wire" barbs' She's (*I'm* is correct as is) "Jacob's Ring" "Wow!" you? (OR you!) You've lovers'

UNIT 9: PUNCTUATION: Comma
Comma in a Series
PRACTICE (pg. 95)
1a. 2 **1b.** 1 **2a.** The blue tree, the yellow bush, and **2b.** mud, bricks, and
YOUR TURN (pg. 96)
1. homework, dyed their hair, stayed out late, and
2a. 1 **2b.** 2
3a. We ate the lemon meringue and strawberry cream pies.
3b. We ate the lemon meringue, strawberry, and cream pies. (OR the lemon, meringue, and strawberry cream)
3c. We ate the lemon, meringue, strawberry, and cream pies.
4. I have only one sister and one brother. One day we were all playing with our two cousins. We ran through four places as fast as we could. They were the hall closet, bedroom, kitchen, and bathroom. Dad was mad at Betty, Joe, and me. He was not mad at my cousins, Mary Sue and Dave. (Mary Sue and Dave should have no commas. Since there are two cousins, Mary Sue must be one of them while the other is Dave. That means "Betty, Joe, and me" refers to the three whose father is mad.)
CHALLENGE (pg. 97)
1a. A.J.'s socks **1b.** A.J.
2a. You'll get watermelon peel, apples, and tie straps. (3 items)
2b. You'll get watermelon, peel apples, and tie straps. (3 actions)
3. (No changes in [1] or [2].) [3]He put the frog on the dog leash, himself in the pond, and the dog on

his bike. ⁴The frog chased a car, stick, squirrel, and two birds. ⁵The dog wobbled down the street, ran into a tree, and fell off. ⁶Josh made a "ribbit" sound, hopped off a rock, fell through a lily pad, and ended up soaked.

Commas to Set Off the Year
PRACTICE (pg. 98)
1a. January 1, 2003, **1b.** December 1, 2002
2a. 1 **2b.** 2
YOUR TURN (pg. 99)
1a. 1842, **1b.** 1960, **1c.** 2020,
2a. April 30, 1945. **2b.** June 23, 1923.
2c. September 19, 2000.
3a. 2 **3b.** 1 **3c.** 2 **3d.** 1
4a. No **4b.** It is the shortened form for a year; the apostrophe stands for the first two digits of the date, probably 19.
CHALLENGE (pg. 100)
1. November 15, 2000, (and) June 10, 2002. (In the last sentence, 2000 is used as part of the nickname "2000 Homer," since we know the year is 2002.)
2a. 2 **2b.** 1 (In b, the comma stands for the words "and the town had".)
3. May 1, 1880.   September 30, 900 people   September 29, 1902, when   In July, 1800 new   January 1, 1903, so

Comma in Address
PRACTICE (pg.101)
1a. 125 Davis Street, Porterstown, California
2. ⓑ
YOUR TURN (pg. 102)
1. Wariner Way, Lovell's Place, Wyoming.
2. 2000 Iz Way, Outatown, Maryland.
3. Clue 1: b Clue 2: c
4. Cordova Boulevard, Fig Springs, California
13 1/2 Sycamore Drive, Pinkertown, Arizona
1445 Country Lane, Baldwin, Maine
CHALLENGE (pg. 103)
1. 222 East Marble Heights, Kentucky Spring West, Virginia
2. 20 Cabbage, Smithville, Maine.
3. 1345 Jerry Way, Atlanta, Georgia
45 Cedar Street, Dobbs Ferry, Texas,
888 Ginger Place, Abbsbury, Utah
690 West Drive, East Carthage, New Jersey

Comma After State
PRACTICE (pg. 104)
1. ⓑ, ⓒ **2b.** New York, New York, **2c.** Galveston, Texas, **2d.** Lake Placid, New York,
YOUR TURN (pg. 105)
1. ⓑ
2a. 1 **2b.** 2
3a. Did you know Alaska is a cold state?
3b. Juneau, Alaska, is a northern city.
3c. He was caught in Parker City, Arizona.
3d. Michael, California is a great state.
CHALLENGE (pg. 105)
1a. Dallas, Texas   **1b.** Dallas, Texas,
1c. Monterey, California,
1d. Monterey, California is
2a. The first sentence means that Bob got Georgia in a swamp. The second means Bob got his frog in a swamp in Huntsville in the state of Georgia.
2b. The first sentence means that they are visiting Bob in a town in Virginia later. The second means that they are visiting Bob in Peakesville today and that they will visit Virginia later in Appleton.

Comma With Noun of Address
PRACTICE (pg. 106)
1. ⓐ, ⓒ (You can tell by the comma before or after Will.) **2a.** 2 **2b.** 1 **3.** ⓑ
YOUR TURN (pg. 107)
1a. 2 **1b.** 1 **1c.** 1 **1d.** 2
2a. Some people have given Ben a failing grade (or they failed him in another way).
2b. You are telling Ben that some other people failed.
3a. This means you should try asking Dad if we may do it.
3b. You are telling Dad that he should try skydiving.
CHALLENGE (pg. 107)
1a. I went to a girl named Dorothy and said, "Dorothy, has your bicycle been broken for long? John has your bicycle in his garage. I saw Gladys fixing it."
1b. She said, "No, Theodore, that was not my bike. Jeremiah has one just like it. Maybe it was his."

The Language Mechanic — Answer Key

1c. "It couldn't have <u>been</u> <u>Jeremiah's</u> bike," said Tootsie. "I saw his bike rolling down the street. He was on <u>it</u>, Dorothy!"

Comma to Separate Quotation From Speaker
PRACTICE (**pg. 108**, corresponding to Your Turn Parts A, B, C)
1a. home," **1b.** case," he said, **2a.** excited!"
2b. exclaimed, **3.** a (no comma after the)
YOUR TURN: Part A (**pg. 109**)
1. ⓒ
2. a is incorrect.
3. <u>ones</u>," he replied. "<u>No</u>," she answered. <u>time</u>," she said.
YOUR TURN: Part B (**pp. 109–110**)
1. ⓑ ⓒ
2a. (correct) **2b.** <u>asked</u>, "Where **2c.** <u>Towville</u>!" he **2d.** <u>begin</u>?" she **2e.** <u>shouted</u>, "It's
3. a <u>wimp</u>!" Lane
<u>calmly</u>, "I
<u>sure</u>?" she
<u>did</u>?" he asked.
YOUR TURN: Part C (**pg. 110**)
1a. 3 **1b.** 1 **1c.** 2
2. c. Mark said, "<u>The Gettysburg Address was given by Lincoln.</u>"
3a. She <u>said</u>, "The **3b.** <u>heaven</u>," sung Mary.
CHALLENGE (**pg. 111**)
1a. She <u>said</u>, "The Rose
1b. I <u>asked</u>, "Which story   He <u>said</u>, "It was
1c. "The <u>Coast</u>," he said.
1d. He <u>chanted</u>, "Wipe   <u>face</u>," as she
2a. 1 **2b.** 2
3. to <u>read</u> "Terror   he <u>sings</u>, "Never
I asked <u>Monica</u>, "Where   call<u>ed</u> "Going South."
In the play," <u>I said</u>, "I think   She <u>said</u>, "Well
finished telling "Terror at Sea."   mate <u>said</u>, "It's
"Oh, I get <u>it</u>!" Monica laughed.

Comma After Introductory Words
PRACTICE (**pg. 112**)
1a. Yes, **1b.** No, **1c.** Well, **1d.** Yes, **2.** ⓑ
YOUR TURN (**pg. 113**)
1a. <u>Yes</u>, I have a pencil.
1b. <u>No</u>, I don't have a book.
2a. (correct) **2b.** <u>Yes</u>, we learn them fast and well.

3. ⓑ (The mother is answering No. The reason is that bones are easily broken.)
4a. Yes (You should leave the dogs at home because *no* dogs are allowed here.)
4b. No (You should not leave the dogs home because dogs *are* allowed here.)
CHALLENGE (**pg. 114**)
1a. 2 **1b.** 1
2. <u>Yes</u>, a person   <u>However</u>, it doesn't   <u>Well</u>, it's
<u>Suddenly</u>, you have   <u>Yes</u>, you have

Comma With Conjunctions
PRACTICE (**pg. 115**)
1. ⓐ We had <u>lunch</u>, we ate all the cookies
2. c He rode into <u>town</u>, and she left.
YOUR TURN (**pg. 116**)
1a. He will run <u>them</u>, or she will run them.
1b. She must come <u>today</u>, or we will be sad.
1c. They tripped the <u>boy</u>, and my cousin fell.
1d. I am ready for <u>fun</u>, and he is ready for work.
2a. 2 **2b.** 1 **2c.** 1 **2d.** 2
3. a. You read our <u>lesson</u>, but we're confused.
(In b, *were* is the past tense verb form: You *were* confused.)
4a. 1 **4b.** 2
CHALLENGE (**pg. 117**)
1a. Without the comma, you'll see him do both the running and the biking. With the comma, you see him run, and you bike down.
1b. Without the comma, he was unable to climb up for the purpose of seeing down below. With the comma, he was able to see down below for the reason that he could not climb up. (The view must have been better from below.)
1c. Without the comma, Jack and John are two different people. She thinks Jack is away, yet she thinks John is home. With the comma, John could be Jack's real name. She thinks he is away, but he is really home. (It could also be a different person; though she thinks Jack is away, another guy named John, is actually at home.)

Commas With Appositives—Words That Explain
PRACTICE (**pg. 118**)
1. <u>c</u> **2a.** 2 **2b.** 1
YOUR TURN (**pg. 119**)
1a. The first sentence is incorrect.

The Language Mechanic — Answer Key

1b. The second sentence is incorrect.
2a. (correct)
2b. Felix gave his father, a black cat, a surprise. (Felix's father, and therefore Felix, is a black cat.) Also acceptable: Felix gave his father a black cat, a surprise. (Be sure that the student understands that the appositive, *a surprise*, refers to *cat* rather than *father* in this sentence.)
3a. 1 **3b.** 2 **3c.** 1 **3d.** 2
4. b

CHALLENGE (pg. 120)
1.ⓑ (means we gave the monkey to her friend)
1.ⓒ (means I put a lot of spicy beans on the food)
2a. 1 **2b.** 2
3a. Rascal, my favorite mutt, was whining at the door. We three, Sis, Rascal, and I, watched the show.
3b. He chased the biggest cars, Cadillacs, with his two pals, Ring and Spot. He gave his friend, a shepherd, a happy bark.
3c. Rascal looked at his dish, an empty bowl. He looked at his owners, Sis and me. His favorite treat, a dog biscuit, was placed in his bowl.

Comma With Introductory Dependent Clause
PRACTICE (pg. 121)
1a. eat, **1b.** light, **1c.** frown, **2.** a is incorrect
YOUR TURN (pg. 122)
1a. correct as is
1b. After it rained, we went out.
1c. Since we were ready, we went swimming.
1d. correct as is
2a. Since he left, I've missed him.
2b. While we were catching toads, I had fun.
3a. 1 **3b.** 2
4a. the pitcher, a ball **4b.** the bull, Bob
5. Sentence *a* tells when you have to pay to be a partner. Sentence *b* tells when you'll be a partner if you pay.
CHALLENGE (pg. 123)
1a. After it rains, out the worms come. (The worms come out after it rains.)
1b. After it rains out, the worms come. (The worms come after it rains outside.) OR After it rains out the worms, come. (Once the worms are washed away, you should come here.)
2a. When you bring your skateboard, we can go to the park. Unless it's raining, we'll use the outdoor skate ramp. If it is raining, we can use the new inside ramp. As soon as I learn it, I'll have to show my brother, Dan. If I know him, he'll be really jealous!
2b. After I land, I'm so proud of myself. Since you've been teaching me, I'm almost as good as Dan.
2c. After I master the basic moves, I want to learn to do flips. Before I try that, maybe I should get some life insurance!

UNIT REVIEW: Comma (pp. 124-5)
June 1995
I rush up the steep hillside, and I look over the top. The cane would slip on the rocks, or it would sink in the mud as she climbed.
I run down the path to the park at 123 East Drive, Carson, New York. All I see is a young gardener bending over the flowers, rocks, and shrubs.
"No, I didn't see anyone," a voice replies from under a large hat. The gardener turns, rises, and walks away. I still can't see the face, but something is familiar. "Excuse me, Sir," I say. The gardener doesn't look back, but points upward. It tells me that it was built on February 1, 1955, and that I am in the "Garden of Youth." I read aloud, "The young become wise, and the old become young."
I see yellow lace lying by a cane, and I suddenly understand.
I am not sure, but I know one thing. I am coming back to the park in Carson, New York, when I get old.

May 2060
It is now February 1, 2060, and I move very slowly. I feel a chill, so I wrap my blue sweater around me. I pick up my cane as I head out of my house at 22 King Street, Carson, New York. I almost fall as my cane dances off the sidewalk, a slippery sheet of cement. After pulling my sweater tight, I struggle up the slope.
No, it's probably my imagination.
"The plants are lovely," I say to myself. I stoop to smell the flowers, a mixture of pinks and

purples. I can feel my <u>aches</u>, <u>pains</u>, and other ailments leaving my body!

"Did you see that old <u>woman</u>, Miss?" a breathless boy is saying to me.

UNIT 10: FRIENDLY LETTER
Capitals and Punctuation in Greeting and Closing (and Body)

PRACTICE (pg. 126)
1. <u>c</u> 2a. 1 2b. 2

PRACTICE (pg. 127)
1a. 2 1b. 1

YOUR TURN (pg. 128)
Note: The answers include only parts of a complete letter format.

1a. Rewrite first line:
My Dear Albert,
Does everything for me have to be difficult?

1b. Rewrite second line:
My Dearest Sofia,
Has a lovely picture come for me? Bring it soon.
                Love,
                George

1c. Rewrite first line:
You haven't been here for days. I hope to see you today.
                Eagerly,
                Manny

2. ⓐ I'd love to be a writer. That's what I plan to be.
                Your friend,
                Jasper

3. Dear Tommy,
We loved your play. We all laughed hard! Let us know when you'll do it again.
                Sincerely,
                Jenny

CHALLENGE (pg. 129)
1a. 2 1b. 1
Dear Mr. Sparkles,
Plants are dying. What should I do?
                Sincerely,
                Mahesh

2. ⓑ is correct

2a. Dear Jake,
I hope someone is having a good time skiing. I'm not.
                Yours truly,
                Mag

3. My dear cousin Ann is naming her new dog after me! She doesn't think her dad will like him. When he sees him, he will love Cary.
(In this version, Ann is the cousin. She is naming her dog Cary.)

Alternative:
My Dear Cousin,
Ann is naming her new dog after me! She doesn't think her dad will like him. When he sees him, he will.
                Love,
                Cary
(In this version, Cary is writing to her cousin. Ann is a different person who is naming her dog after Cary.)

UNIT REVIEW: Friendly Letter (pg. 130)

                September 15, 2005
Dear Mamie**,**
<u>We</u> wish you could see the beautiful sky here! It looks like someone painted it! The sun almost bleeds into the surrounding blue. The puffy clouds are like cotton absorbing the orange and pink. We'll bring you a photograph soon.
                <u>Love</u>**,**
                <u>Lonny and Tyke</u>

                October 1, 3050
<u>My Dearest Eduardo</u>**,**
<u>Please</u> consider my suggestion. We are from two different planets, but that shouldn't matter. You could get used to living on Tarmon. I'm sure you understand why I can't live on your planet of Swarmagon <u>eaters</u>.
                <u>Your Swarmagon</u>**,**
                <u>Snooki</u>

UNIT 11: SPELLING AND VOCABULARY

Confused Word Pairs
PRACTICE (pg. 131)
1a. lie, lay **1b.** sets, sits **1c.** can, may **1d.** teach, learn **1e.** lend, borrow **1f.** leave, let **1g.** rise, raise
YOUR TURN (pg. 133)
1a. 1 **1b.** 2
2a. let, leave **2b.** raise, rise **2c.** sit, set
3a. He lays his head down as he <u>lies</u> in bed.
3b. He may have a cookie if he <u>can</u> reach it.
CHALLENGE (pg. 133)
1a. 2 **1b.** 1
2a. lay, lie **2b.** lies, lays, lies, lies

Homophones and Other Similar Words
PRACTICE (pg. 134)
1a. for, four **1b.** to, two, too **1c.** hear, here
1d. it's, its **1e.** there, their **1f.** see, sea **1g.** son, sun **1h.** are, our
YOUR TURN (pg. 136)
1. ⓑ
2a. here **2b.** hear **2c.** see **2d.** sea
3a. to, two, too **3b.** it's, its **3c.** there, their
3d. rays, raise **3e.** are, our
4a. 1 **4b.** 2
CHALLENGE (pg. 137)
1a. They got their first plate, and they'll get another later.
1b. They got there first because they were fastest.
2a. 2 **2b.** 1
3a. Whoever is being spoken to has teachers for parents. **3b.** All the people mentioned are actors (parents, teachers, and cousins).
4. knot: He did tie the rope, by making a knot.
not: He did not tie the rope.
5. Answers will vary

Spelling Plural and Singular Nouns
PRACTICE (pg. 138)
1a. girl, girls **1b.** fox, foxes **1c.** men, man
1d. life, lives **1e.** sheep, sheep **1f.** babies, baby
YOUR TURN (pg. 139)
1a. snake, sticks **1b.** snacks, buddies
1c. puppies, mother **1d.** sheep, sheep
2a. women **2b.** men **2c.** children

3. fish, fish; deer, deer
4a. knife **4b.** knives
5. b, c, f are correct.
5a. foxes **5d.** watches **5e.** leaves
CHALLENGE (pg. 140)
1a. loaves **1b.** loafs, loaf
2a. leaf **2b.** leave, leaves
3. skies, party, goodies, buddies OR enemies, beauty

Silent Consonants
PRACTICE (pg.141)
1. ring, wring **2a.** knight **2b.** night **3a.** Nat, gnat
3b. hour, our **3c.** knot, not
YOUR TURN (pg. 143)
1a. 1 **1b.** 2
2a. not, knot **2b.** not, knot **2c.** our **2d.** hour
2e. whole **2f.** hole
3. nice, knew, knife, know, no, Now
CHALLENGE (pg. 143)
1. writes, rites
2a. wrings: He squeezes out the collar.
rings: He circles or puts a ring around the collar.
2b. knot: I would make a knot in the rope.
not: I would leave the rope tied.

Silent E for Long Vowels
PRACTICE (pg. 144)
1a. rid, ride **1b.** can, cane **1c.** win, wine
1d. mate, mat
YOUR TURN (pg. 145)
1a. rat, rate **1b.** can, cane **1c.** ride, rid
1d. mate, mat **1e.** win, wine
2a. 1 **2b.** 2
CHALLENGE (pg. 145)
1a. You could survive by living off your *fat*. You could also depend on *fate*, or luck.
1b. You could build a flying toy using a *kit*. You could also get a *kite*.
1c. You could pick up sugar that is in a *can*. You could also pick up a stalk of sugar *cane*.
2. New words: bite, ate, cute, made, hate, note, site. Sentences will vary.

Consonant Doubling With -ing or -ed
PRACTICE (pg. 146)
1. fan, bat, sun, rig **2a.** bid, bidding **2b.** tagged,

tag **2c.** robbing **2d.** ridded, rid
YOUR TURN (pg. 147)
1a. 2 **1b.** 1
2. b, c
3. whipped, sitting, cutting, topping
4a. wagged, waged **4b.** fatted, fated
CHALLENGE (pg. 147)
1a. 2 **1b.** 1
2a. If you have a disgusting hairdo, you could *hate* it (dislike it), and you might *hat* it (cover it with a hat) so you don't have to see it.
2b. You would have to *hop* in a sack race. You can also *hope* that you will win.

UNIT REVIEW: Spelling and Vocabulary (pp. 148–9)

I am nervous. This will be my first real game of 3-D batball. We are about to play against the Divers, who beat our team last season. The Eagles just *have* to win this time. I can't let them down!

Playing in three dimensions isn't easy. First, you have to be good at floating and gliding. Most people can do this, but don't know it. Second, you have to be good at batting a ball. The Eagles taught me to put the two skills together. The whole team would hit easy shots to me so I could bat the ball while flying. Then we'd play faster and harder until I was good. That was practice. Now I will play against real players. Men, women, and children will be watching me.

The sun shines brightly as the game begins. We play well, cutting the air like knives as we swoop and turn. We quickly make two goals. Then Callahan, our fastest player, fouls out. She has to sit down for the rest of the game! We're down to four players. The Divers catch up by hitting one, then two balls into the goal.

I see a flicker to my left, and I dive for it. False alarm! The ball whizzes by to the right. The Divers get it and take it easily to the goal! I'd better not react so quickly next time. Again, I hear the ball whiz by above me. I see it too late! Sheliah and Jose shake their heads at me in disgust. I almost decide that I'm not cut out for this game. The the skies darken with clouds, and I grow confident. That's because I usually practice at night!

I see the ball coming fast. I raise my bat as I eye the goal. Can I hit that far? Cory yells, "It's out of bounds! Leave it alone!" I ignore him. I give it all I've got. It flies into the goal! It's just what the Eagles needed to get going. Next, Sheliah slides the ball to Cory right under a Diver's nose and passes it to Jose. He makes another goal! We have become quick and clever like foxes. The Divers have become like sheep who seem confused and slow.

A diver is about to pass the ball to her partner. I rise up and surprise her. She almost lets go of her bat! I pass the ball to Cory, who takes it to the goal. Winning is like taking candy from babies!

The Eagles pat me on the back. "You were great! You were our knight in shining armor!" they say. "Thanks, but may I make a suggestion?" I say. We should either practice in the daytime or have our matches at night!"

Punctuation Puzzlers   Sample Activity

> Tickle your funny bone while tackling punctuation and other language skills—in the amazingly fun *Punctuation Puzzlers*. There are 3 three levels: A, Grades 3–4; B, Grades 5–6; and C, Grades 7–8. Use these books as a fun way to apply the lessons learned in *The Language Mechanic*!

Comma Series: Action

12. The picture shows the meaning of the sentence. Add the commas needed to correct it.

    We go to the barn see the cows square dance and leave.

13. Find the meaning of the sentences. Add the commas needed to correct them.

    **We go to the barn see the cows square dance and leave.
    The cows are asleep the whole time.**

RULE: In a series of three or more items, place a comma after each item except the last. *She goes home, shuts the door, and reads a book.*

172   © 2001 The Critical Thinking Co.™ • www.CriticalThinking.com • 800-458-4849